Beyond Missionaries

Religious Forces in the Modern Political World
General Editor Allen D. Hertzke, The Carl Albert Center, University of Oklahoma at Norman

Religious Forces in the Modern Political World features books on religious forces in politics, both in the United States and abroad. The authors examine the complex interplay between religious faith and politics in the modern world, emphasizing its impact on contemporary political developments. This new series spans a diverse range of methodological interpretations, philosophical approaches, and substantive concerns. Titles include:

Beyond Missionaries

Toward an Understanding of the Protestant Movement in Central America

Anne Motley Hallum

ROWMAN & LITTLEFIELD PUBLISHERS, INC.
Lanham · Boulder · New York · London

ROWMAN & LITTLEFIELD PUBLISHERS, INC.

Published in the United States of America
by Rowman & Littlefield Publishers, Inc.
4720 Boston Way, Lanham, Maryland 20706
3 Henrietta Street
London, WC2E 8LU, England

British Cataloging in Publication Information Available

Library of Congress Cataloging-in-Publication Data

Hallum, Anne M.
The fullness of time : toward an understanding of the Protestant
Movement in Central America / Anne M. Hallum.
p.   cm — (Religious forces in the modern political world)
Includes bibliographical references and index.
1. Protestant churches—Central America—History. 2. Central
America—Church history. I. Title. II. Series.
BX4833.5.H35   1996   280'.4'09728—dc20   96-22603 CIP

ISBN 0-8476-8297-8 (cloth : alk. paper)
ISBN 0-8476-8298-6 (pbk. : alk. paper

Printed in the United States of America

∞™ The paper used in this publication meets the minimum requirements of
American National Standard for Information Sciences—Permanence of
Paper for Printed Library Materials, ANSI Z39.48–1984.

Every religion has some political opinion linked to it by affinity.
The spirit of man, left to follow its bent, will regulate political society and the City of God in uniform fashion; it will, if I dare put it so, seek to *harmonize* earth with heaven.

—Alexis de Tocqueville
Democracy in America
Vol. 1, Part II, chapter 9

Contents

Tables and Figures

Preface

The idea for writing this book came to me during my first visit to Central America seven years ago. Even then, I frequently found myself in discussions with tourists and expatriates about religious changes in the region, but I felt uneasy about the strong emotions, opinions, and certitude that pervaded these discussions. The consensus was invariably that U.S. imperialism was at work once again through the missionaries. The people, it was asserted, were being bribed into acceptance and would follow any doctrine or religious formula in order to receive handouts. The scenario continued that Protestant missionaries would bring right-wing politics and that conversion played into the hands of the status quo powers. Furthermore, the critics of Protestantism needed only to talk with some of the short-term missionaries to verify their perspective. Some idealistic summer missionary could always be found, it seemed, praising the idea that Central America would turn into North America's offspring, becoming Protestant, capitalistic, democratic, and Western simultaneously!

It seemed to me that an important movement *was* taking place, but that the most important actors were being altogether left out of the analysis. It also seemed to me the height of elitism for outsiders to discount the genuine enthusiasm of the churchgoers, or to denigrate automatically the religious choices of people who had known so much terror and violent death. I was also frustrated by the almost total neglect by political scientists of this phenomenon which seemed to be a significant challenge to the traditional Catholic hegemony. Eventually I read works by anthropologists David Stoll and David Martin, who were the first to break through the easy assumptions about Protestantism in Central America, and I was encouraged to dig deeper myself. I was traveling frequently to the region to work with the Alliance for International Reforestation, Inc. (A.I.R.), and I began to include more visits to churches, to talk to the residents about religion at every opportunity, and to live with an evangelical family in Costa Rica for a time. The evangelicals of Central America I encountered were not bribed or brainwashed by the missionaries, nor do they accept the teachings without question or adaptation. Similarly, I learned that leaders of the Catholic Church are not passive bystanders failing to respond to the movement swirling around them. I present these and related observations in this book, placed in the context of social movement theory.

My intellectual acknowledgements regarding research methods and the link between religion and politics go particularly to Alexis de Tocqueville, Max Weber, Clifford Geertz, Daniel Levine, David Stoll, David Martin, and Sydney Tarrow. On a more personal level, I wish to acknowledge my colleagues at Stetson, Phillip Lucas of the Religious Studies Department and Brazilian scholar William Nylen who both read draft chapters and provided valuable comments and support. My earliest, and perhaps most important collegial support came from Allen Hertzke, the general editor of this series. Allen would always greet me at frequent conferences with the same sequence of questions: "How many times have you been there for interviews?" and "Where's your book?" I would patiently explain the problem of weak empirical data, the virtual impossibility of even counting the number of evangelicals, and the lack of interest in the field. But Allen read my conference papers and persisted with his gentle encouragement and eventually, his recommendation that I be included in this series. I am grateful for his confidence and for his insistence that statistical analysis is not the only way to understand social and political change.

I owe a deep debt of gratitude to all the people who took the time to talk with me about religion and politics. Without exception, the respondents were thoughtful, open, insightful, and generous with their time. The names of those who granted formal interviews are given in the reference pages and in chapter endnotes, but my gratitude extends to dozens of anonymous Central Americans who spoke with me informally. I particularly wish to acknowledge Dennis Smith of the Latin America Evangelical Center for Pastoral Studies (CELEP) in Guatemala City, Guatemala.

Dennis met with me several times over a five year period, and I always found him to be highly informed, perceptive, and eloquent. In addition, I could not have conducted the interviews in Nicaragua and El Salvador without the assistance of Guillermo Sutterfield. He has consistently been a source for ideas, argument, encouragement, translation, and friendship throughout the course of this project.

Stetson University supported this work through three research grants which I gratefully acknowledge. Also at Stetson, I am indebted to Robin Carter who efficiently and calmly kept me close to deadlines and to the eminent expertise of reference librarian David Everett. I admire and appreciate the professional staff at Rowman & Littlefield Publishers, particularly Deirdre Mullervy and Stephen Wrinn. They put me in contact with excellent anonymous reviewers and were patient and proficient in accepting manuscript changes.

My daughters, Rachel and Rebecca, were my welcome traveling companions on two trips to Central America and offered their own perspectives on those experiences. My girls have been patient beyond their years with their mother's preoccupation with "the book," and I will always be grateful. Jan, Rachel, and Rebecca have given me unfailing support *and* frequent, rejuvenating distractions. They are my joy.

Anne Motley Hallum

Chapter One

Introduction:
Protestantism as a Social
Movement

Pentecostalism is the movement of the century in Latin America.

— Jorge Bardeguez
Historian, Centroecumenico
Antonio Valdivieso
Managua, Nicaragua, 1993

Some may regard the quotation above as hyperbole, but it does accurately reflect the view on the scene in Central America that the latest wave of conversion to Protestantism—especially the Pentecostal variety—is highly significant. It has been six years since the publication of David Stoll's pathbreaking study, *Is Latin America Turning Protestant? The Politics of Evangelical Growth*, and David Martin's book, *Tongues of Fire: The Explosion of Protestantism in Latin America*.[1] These provocative books explored causes for the growth of Protestantism throughout Latin America and prompted renewed interest in two earlier works by Christian Lalive d'Epinay and Emilio Willems.[2] In the last few years other sociologists have examined the potential *impact* of the phenomenon as well as causes.[3]

However, the political science community has been excruciatingly slow to awaken to the significance and complexity of the Protestant presence in Latin America especially when compared to anthropologists. One political scientist simply admits that "focus on religious identity requires more time and patience than political scientists have" and "[a]nthropologists are on the whole more willing than other social scientists to spend time in poor

1

neighborhoods."[4] This research challenge is not altogether war-
ranted, particularly with regard to the study of Catholicism; but
it is true that the amount of research on political parties, policies, economic structures, or the state far outweighs analysis of
religion in the political science discipline. As Edward Luttwak
observes in a recent book about religion as a factor for international peacemaking, the study of religion has been subjected to
an ancient "Enlightenment prejudice,"[5] which saw religion as a
force of ignorance during the Dark Ages. Thus it was closed, ironically, to intellectual pursuit in the Age of Reason and beyond.
Luttwak laments the long-term implications for scholarship this
exclusionary attitude has produced: those who were writing about
political systems and cultures were deeply estranged from those
who lived in them, i.e., the majorities who were influenced by religion in their politics and who practiced religion daily.

This estrangement was reinforced by Marxist theory, which
labeled religion an "opiate," and by modernization or secularization theories, which predicted that nations would eventually out-
grow religion as they became more literate, industrialized, urban,
and urbane. In the meantime, in this common view, religion was
merely a peripheral factor, an "epiphenomenon."[6] Political science
was particularly obedient to this reasoning. "Religion and Politics" became a recognized division in the American Political Science Association only in the 1980s, a time when the intersection
of religion and politics in presidential politics and in fundamentalist movements around the world had become too obvious to
ignore further.

Political scientists began to venture into concentrated study of
religion in Latin America with analyses of liberation theology in
the 1980s, particularly as practiced by Catholics. This theology,
which inspires courageous challenges to systemic political and
economic evils, is disseminated in scholarly writings by numerous
theologians. It is still practiced in thousands of *comunidades ecle-
siales de base* (CEBs) throughout Latin America and seems particularly amenable to political science purview. The explicitly
intellectual and political aspects of this particular brand of religion were relatively familiar territory for scholars. Daniel Levine,
Scott Mainwaring and Alexander Wilde, among many others, accepted the anthropology challenge to "spend time in poor neigh-

borhoods," as well as in libraries, and produced insightful studies about the power of liberation theology.[7] One 1981 bibliography of works in English about the Catholic progressive church included an astonishing 3,966 entries.[8] Meanwhile, the Protestant movement in Latin America was experiencing growth far more extensive than that stimulated by liberation theology, but it went virtually unnoticed—or at least unpublished—by the academy.[9] Thus, the intellectual blinders of the Enlightenment remained in place as scholars fixated on liberation theology which, in Brazil for instance, only reached 1 or 2 percent of the population, when Protestantism had reached many times that number of people in the same time period.[10] Similar comparisons can be made throughout Latin America. Eurocentric theorizing in the social sciences contributed to this blind spot because the Protestant religion, and religion in general, had arguably become relatively insignificant in European politics, which was somehow assumed to be a universal trend.[11]

When a few scholars broadened their scope to examine Protestant church proliferation, they at first it was most often attributed it to the macrolevel forces of U.S. imperialism and preservation of global economic systems. This perspective is clearly illustrated in the following statement:

> The U.S. evangelicals are coming to Central America with more than Bibles. Many of them bring a pacifying ideology that forgives the guilty and soothes the poor with promises of personal salvation. It is a U.S.-manufactured antidote to liberation and social justice theology. . . . In Central America, the emerging religious right is helping keep reactionary elites in power and may prove a serious obstacle to revolutionary transformations that are long overdue.[12]

This warning now seems a gross oversimplification to those who have been following Protestant developments in the region. For centuries politicians have attempted to use missionaries for their purposes, and in chapter 2 we will review the more brutal recent examples of this opportunism in Central America. But thoughtful research reveals that religion is a force far too complicated to be contained within the best-laid political plans.

Furthermore, writers about Protestantism (as typified in the above quotation) condescendingly assume the people of Latin America to be passive receivers of external attempts to dominate.

In fact, as we shall see throughout this book, the people have pragmatic as well as spiritual arguments for actively choosing or for rejecting Protestantism. If Protestantism is accepted, it is most often reworked, revised, molded, and adapted to the needs of the class and the context where particular churches are situated. The overriding traits of Protestantism in Latin America are diversity and flexibility. The vast majority of these churches are by now under local rather than missionary leadership. If local reworking and adaptations do not take place in a particular church, it will eventually lose members and die. (Some observers have argued that the inability of some liberation theology base communities to adapt to immediate needs and context is one factor accounting for their present stagnation.[13]) Thus the first commitment of this book is to be contextual—to examine specific Protestant categories and the movement in specific countries. We would love to pin down explanatory generalizations about the direction of the Protestant phenomenon in all of Latin America, but useful generalizations are few and far between. This is particularly true in regard to an analysis of the possible impact of the movement. We will most often, then, be comparing recent religious and political impacts in the contexts of five Central American nations.

Fortunately the natural trajectory of scholarly pursuit is gradually leading to more fieldwork and in-depth analysis, primarily by anthropologists, that allows contextual comparisons. The stereotype of Latin American Protestants meekly serving the status quo powers is being refuted by a growing body of Latin American case studies.[14] This book adds a political science perspective to this closer scrutiny in the belief that breaking down disciplinary barriers can aid us in the painstaking breakdown of stereotypes. Ten years ago Daniel Levine pointed out that, whereas political scientists focus on institutions and formal protests, anthropologists focus on phenomena and structures among the masses. Yet the most useful approach is to see institutional and popular dimensions together.[15] Thus the second commitment of this work is to be interdisciplinary, examining both Protestant religious institutions and small religious communities. I have found the social movement literature to be extraordinarily useful for understanding the current Protestant movement in

Central America, as well as anthropology research, survey research, and fieldwork.

The third overriding commitment is to attempt to bridge the separation between those who study politics and those who engage in the acts of everyday life. I quote the following passage from a review essay by Daniel Levine at length because this passage has been a guiding principle for my research:

> To understand how religion and politics interact and change together, analysis must accept the logic of religious belief and practice. This requires a conscious effort to hear it as expressed, to see it as practiced, and to construct or reconstruct the context in which these religious ideas resonate. Only then is it possible to see how and why religion helps people to make sense of the world and to organize themselves and others to deal with it. All this adds up to the need for scholarship to begin with what religious groups and people *actually do,* and not with an account of why they do not do things of interest to social scientists, such as engaging in explicitly political activities.[16]

This analytical approach is intrinsically difficult for political scientists who are focused on macrolevel systems and burdened by "Enlightenment prejudice." It is safe to say that practices of the Pentecostals, for instance, speaking in tongues, or faith healing, and all-night prayer vigils, are completely alien to the average political scientist and thus difficult to analyze. But Pentecostalism is what millions of Latin Americans now actually practice, and Levine suggests that there is a need for scholarship to begin wherever that place might be. I take his advice not as an exclusive endorsement of participant-observer anthropological research but as a recommendation to adjust our attitude whenever we analyze data on the impact of religion—whether it be surveys, aggregate data, interviews, or fieldwork. The adjustment is for us not to prejudge but to "accept the logic of religious belief and practice" to the believers. I recall the personal impact of a statement that was made during an interview in Nicaragua by a preacher attempting to explain to me the essential difference between liberation theology and Pentecostalism: "Liberation theology takes 'a preferential option for the poor', but the Pentecostals *are* the poor." This is not a negation of liberation theology but a reminder that researchers seeking to understand social movements must go where the people lead them.

LESSONS FROM SOCIAL
MOVEMENT THEORY

Numerous fascinating single-case studies on Protestantism in Latin America exist in the anthropology literature. They demonstrate both the importance of context and the difficulty of finding theoretical generalizations. There is a need for overarching analysis from the case studies, and social movement theory can help us identify the useful generalizations and explanations. What are the particular framing mechanisms within Protestantism as a social movement in Central America? What are the particular dynamics of the movement, i.e., will it peak and then evaporate, or will it become routinized in the society? What are its mobilizing structures? Who are the opponents of the movement and how are they responding? Can any predictions be made about the political and cultural impact of Protestantism? What are the most useful ways to make such assessments?

At first gloss, this particular religious phenomenon is difficult to see as a social movement at all for several reasons. First, much early focus examined missionary activity and the imposition of Protestantism rather than the grassroots response to the missionaries. This institutional factor of identifying the founding missions in particular countries is a crucial starting point. However, we will move far beyond initial missionary patterns in this analysis in order to identify movement characteristics. Another difficulty is that Protestantism emphasizes personal religious experiences, and thus it is often characterized as "individualistic," obscuring the community-building that is occurring at many levels. We need to remember, for instance, that private and public lives are seldom as separated for most Latin Americans as they are for North Americans. A "private" conversion experience, for instance, will be widely shared in an experience of bonding with a large community.

It has also been a struggle for scholars to see Protestantism as a social movement because they usually emphasize the state as the opposing force, insisting that it is the "fundamental referent" for gauging the development and success of social movements.[17] Therefore, since Protestantism is in opposition to secularization and Catholicism, the theoretical emphasis on the state as referent might logically exclude Protestantism as a social movement.

However, this ignores the fact that church and state are not separated in Latin America. Traditionally Catholicism has been closely aligned with the state, so the opposing Protestants sometimes implicitly oppose the state. At other times they may join Catholic progressives in an alliance against the state. On the other hand, Central American governments have been an ally of Protestants at times, as in the mid-1800s to early 1900s when liberal governments encouraged Protestant worship as a counter to Catholic hegemony, or in the 1970s and 1980s when Protestant missionary aid was solicited by the state. Ultimately, however, and in the deeper sense asserted by the Reformation, religion is always properly in opposition to the state because its adherents swear allegiance to a higher authority than government. Thus religious actors often have been "voices in the wilderness" in the prophetic sense of announcing to the powers of the state criticisms that they did not want to hear.[18] The degree of tension between the state and the Protestants varies widely over time and among these five countries, as we shall see in chapters 4 and 5.

Finally, political scientists have been slow to see Protestantism as a social movement because religion (like feminist movements) involves "[S]truggles over meanings at the level of daily life," and too often "daily life has been rendered invisible or secondary by conventional social sciences."[19] Protestantism in Latin America is decidedly still in formation, and sensitive scrutiny at the level of everyday life is necessary to assess its power as a movement.

Political scientist Sidney Tarrow (inspired by French historian Charles Tilly) provides a practical definition of social movements: "collective challenges by people with common purposes and solidarity in sustained interaction with elites, opponents and authorities."[20] These challenges may be to cultural codes, Tarrow explains, and they include "collective affirmation of new values" or what Rhys Williams calls "alternative cultural arrangements."[21] Either phrase would encompass Protestantism in Latin America. Objections might arise over defining Protestantism as a "collective" due to its fragmentation into hundreds of denominations and faith missions. However, I would argue strongly from my observations that the depth of this fragmentation has been overstated and that, in any case, diversity is actually a strength of the movement. Protestant variety allows persons with many different approaches to religion to find a church where they are comfortable but they can unite with other church members in a collective identity. The "movement" aspect of Protestantism became gradually clearer to me as I broached the subject of religion countless times with persons on the street. Invariably, the person's first response was to ask enthusiastically if I were a Protestant, always using the generic Protestant labels of "an evangelical?" or "a Christian?" or simply, "a sister?" The questioner was not interested in my particular denomination; rather the priority was to identify if I *belonged* to the broad movement or if I was a Catholic or secular outsider.

Our purpose here is to examine *how* Protestantism is coalescing into an authentic movement and what the implications might be for the region. These implications are coming to light gradually because this religious alternative began strictly as an artificial import. It has been noted that in Latin America, unlike Europe, "cultural and economic forms of different temporal origins coexist, forming layers rather than stages."[22] Protestantism is now widespread enough to be considered one of the layers, both influencing and being influenced by other layers. The overall assertion—broader than the Weberian tradition that focuses on economics—is that religious choices are not merely isolated, individualistic and private, but will eventually matter for the encompassing societies.

Movement Recruitment

As a starting point for understanding movement recruitment, chapter 2 examines original U.S. missionary patterns as the institutional source for Protestantism in the region, but only as the catalyst for the actual movement. In social movement terms the missionaries were, and are, "external interventions"; however, as Arturo Escobar notes, and as we shall see throughout the book, such interventions do not negate the autonomy and tight community-building of a movement.[23]

Chapter 2 also provides background on the extent of Protestantism in Central America, insofar as data exists. The unreliability of estimates about the growth of Protestantism reflects practical hardships in gathering data. It also demonstrates the threat posed by the movement to the status quo. Opponents of Protestantism minimize its growth, whereas proponents tend to exaggerate its success. In discussing North American involvement, we will address the calculated use of missionaries by the U.S. government. Missionaries provided a convenient network for transmission of U.S. foreign policy objectives. This additional intervention compounded the artificiality of Protestantism in Latin America, hurt its credibility among the people, and slowed the process of movement formation.

Considering its ignoble beginnings, why has Protestantism turned into an authentic social movement in Central America? Tarrow stresses the importance of seizing opportunities: "Social movements form when ordinary citizens, sometimes encouraged by leaders, respond to changes in opportunities that lower the costs of collective action, reveal potential allies and show where elites and authorities are vulnerable."[24] The "changes in opportunities" that people have responded to in Central America are numerous: changing political regimes, economic crises, and cultural conflicts. Leaders in Central America have quietly encouraged Protestant missionaries in the face of their state's incapacity to meet the most basic needs of the vast majority of their people, thus providing the missionaries with a particular opportunity.

More often than not, the governments have come to recognize the resources in social welfare that are attached to missionary organizations. This is most evident in the face of emergencies such as earthquakes and hurricanes when the governments desperately welcome the now predictable influx of missionaries. But the state's need for church help is not limited to emergencies. In Guatemala, for instance, the National Reconstruction Commission of the Guatemalan government attempts to coordinate the work of hundreds of nongovernmental organizations, and the vast majority of the projects it has registered are sponsored by Protestant churches.[25] The Catholic Church remains an invaluable resource for social programs, but the Protestants are equally supportive and thus governments invite them. This open-door policy to charities is in tandem with the neoliberal approach of less state involvement in social and economic reforms, an approach pushed on Central America by international agencies and by changes in the international economy. An interesting and potentially significant side effect has been the dilemma that some elected officials have come to face. They need churches to provide numerous welfare and development functions in the face of state incapacity. But these same officials are unable to control the autonomous religious bodies, and they may turn into the state's harshest critics. We will discuss early signs of this occurring in Guatemala and Nicaragua.

We reject the "mass society" tradition of sociology that would explain movement development as the collective behavior of disoriented individuals in a rapidly modernizing world. In this view the movement participants are seen as an undifferentiated populace and are recruited almost as victims of "religious" demagogues.[26] In chapter 2 and parts of chapter 3, we shall demonstrate that the process of recruitment has moved largely beyond missionary contacts, occurring most often in social networks of face-to-face interaction with friends and family members. The reasons for choosing Protestantism are not mass "anomie," nor are they necessarily "rational" in the terms of a calculating economic rational-choice theory, but they are certainly pragmatic and understandable for the individuals involved.

Movement Mobilization

Chapter 3 focuses sharply on identifying the actors and the movement resources they are developing. We shall outline theological teachings and shall define three broad categories of Protestants in Central America in an attempt to make the scores of denominations and faith missions understandable. Identifying three categories allows us to make some generalizations about possible political implications. The categorization reveals some internal dynamics of the movement because the Protestant groupings vary in strength and philosophy. Protestantism in Latin America is not monolithic, but neither is it hopelessly fragmented, and thus lacking the potential of a social movement.

Chapter 3 also illustrates the process of "framing," i.e., providing meaning to a social movement through common symbols and understandings. A recurring theme in Tarrow's work is the importance of literacy and printing to the original phenomena of social movements because it is through broad sharing of the printed word that people discover their common causes. In the case of Protestantism it is not doctrine or creeds that are important for framing; rather, frequent study of particular passages in the Bible have helped to mobilize the movement, as we shall see. Underscoring this point, we note Daniel Levine's observation that "[a]ccess to the Bible is utterly new in the popular religious culture of Latin America. Mass literacy is of course recent, and in any event, earlier generations were taught that reading the Bible was more than simply unnecessary: it was forbidden."[27] In contrast to the Catholic tradition of leaving Bible reading to the clergy, Protestant practice has promoted widespread access to the Bible. (Witness the work of Wycliffe Bible Translators, who have almost completed translating the Bible into twenty-two Mayan dialects in Guatemala, begun decades ago.) The spread of Protestantism in Latin America would seem to confirm Tarrow's emphasis on the importance of common, printed words for movement mobilization. This movement is what Robert Wuthnow has called a "community of discourse" that serves as the carrier of a set of core ideas—ideas about moral behavior, the need to support the community of fellow believers, and the certainty of God's plan for his kingdom.[28] It is an ideology gleaned from a particular way of reading, discussing, and experiencing the Bible.

Movement Opponents

Chapter 4 focuses on Catholic-Protestant tensions, since Catholics are the primary force of opposition to Protestantism at this point. We will examine religious interactions in each of the five countries for context and present a typology of confrontation, compromise, or cooperation. The Catholic-Protestant relationship is evolving in a few different ways and provides a portrayal of how elites and authorities react to the challenging collective action of a movement.

The explicitly political outcomes of the Protestant movement in Central America are speculative at this point, but the impact of the movement on Catholic hegemony in the region is undeniable. The most recent Latin American Bishops Conference proclaimed that one of the major challenges to the Catholic Church in the coming millennium is combating the spread of other churches in Latin America. The bishops condemned what they called "soul trafficking" in the region and reported that "two Catholics are leaving the Church every 30 minutes."[29] Not all members of the Catholic hierarchy are confrontational with the evangelicals; some have a more cooperative, ecumenical response than the conference report indicates. The point is that this institution, which has been at the center of power in Latin America for centuries, is being seriously challenged and is responding. It is true that the Catholic hierarchy has denounced "the invasion of the sects" many times before in Latin America, but now, in the 1980s and 1990s, the conversion rates are strong enough that denunciation of the evangelicals is being combined with both retrenchment and creative reforms. In the unlikely event that the Protestant movement becomes routinized and fades tomorrow, the impact it has already had on the Catholic Church is significant in and of itself. In a real sense it has expanded cultural and religious alternatives in a region where one church has held a virtual monopoly for centuries.

Movement Institutionalization

In the dynamics of social movements the stage of institutionalization is fraught with risk because participants often lose sight of their common cause as they become concerned instead with maintaining organizations. Extraordinary creativity and leadership are necessary to maintain momentum and to exert an impact on the broader society. A large majority of the Central American pastors are by now natives, without missionary ties. Several Protestant theological seminaries and research institutes are well established there, and even the highly spiritual Pentecostal leaders are beginning to seek formal training. In chapters 5 and 6 I bring together various threads of the analysis by showing how Protestantism in Central America is now entering a phase of institutionalization that raises the possibility of greater political involvement. I assess possible political outcomes of Protestantism primarily in Guatemala and Nicaragua, where Protestant political parties are forming. The differences in the two countries, which are at the nexus of Protestantism and politics, demonstrate the importance of context for analyzing local as well as presidential politics.

Furthermore, I argue that assessing these differences in the political direction of the Protestant movement requires analysis of three factors: founding missionary patterns in each country (i.e., the institutional source), local leadership dynamics, and particular political cultures. The contrasts between Guatemala and Nicaragua will illustrate the significance of variations in these factors. I will also explore political ramifications and early signs that Protestantism may be most challenging not at the presidential level but in the form of a local populism that combats government corruption in villages and towns. As Protestantism in Central America comes of age with its own national institutions, leaders, and devotees, we can begin to analyze these broader implications.

Research is based on literature review and interviews conducted between 1990 and 1995 in over a dozen trips to Central America. The interviews include elite interviews with religious and political leaders in Guatemala, Costa Rica, El Salvador, and Nicaragua, as well as innumerable conversations with vendors, taxi drivers, churchgoers, and anyone else who wanted to talk about personal religious experiences, which people appear very willing to do in Central America. For research purposes I also attended a school for U.S. missionaries in Costa Rica and lived with a generous and gracious evangelical family during that time. In addition, I am fortunate to head a small nonprofit environmental organization in Guatemala, which gives me ready access to many villages in Guatemala where we work. Getting to know the Catholics and Protestants who work with us on environmental projects has also been invaluable for opening my understanding of religious/cultural developments. As any close observer of Protestantism in Central America quickly learns, the label "evangelical" is used more often than "Protestant." It refers to any non-Catholic Christian except the quasi-Christian Mormons and Jehovah's Witnesses, who practice a distinct theology. This work will therefore use "evangelical" interchangeably with "Protestant."

Sociologists David Martin and David Stoll surveyed existing research in their 1990 analyses of Protestantism in Latin America. Sufficient research has been published since that time to warrant an updated survey of the literature within the present analysis, particularly since the movement is entering a new phase of becoming more institutionalized. As we shall see, Protestantism began when state leaders encouraged opportunities for its growth; it has been successful in framing itself in ways that allow for mobilization, particularly in poorer communities; and it is entering a phase of institutionalization that raises the possibility of greater political involvement. The particular direction of that involvement depends on varying missionary histories, leadership development, and political cultures. Thus we are examining a movement in process. As in any scholarly pursuit, revisionism, analytical updates, and open minds are appropriate.

NOTES

1. David Stoll, *Is Latin America Turning Protestant? The Politics of Evangelical Growth* (Berkeley: University of California Press, 1990); David Martin, *Tongues of Fire: The Explosion of Protestantism in Latin America* (London: Blackwell, 1990).

2. Christian Lalive d'Epinay, *Haven to the Masses: A Study of the Pentecostal Movement in Chile* (London: Lutterworth, 1969); Emilio Willems, *Followers of the New Faith: Culture Change and the Rise of Protestantism in Brazil and Chile* (Nashville: Vanderbilt University Press, 1967).

3. The majority of scholarship on Protestantism in Latin America has been produced by anthropologists. In addition to those cited above, see Sheldon Annis, *God and Production in a Guatemala Town* (Austin: University of Texas Press, 1987); Virginia Garrard-Burnett and David Stoll, eds., *Rethinking Protestantism in Latin America* (Philadelphia: Temple University Press, 1993); Rowan Ireland, *Kingdoms Come: Religion and Politics in Brazil* (Pittsburgh: University of Pittsburgh Press, 1991); Cecilia Loreto Mariz, *Coping with Poverty: Pentecostals and Christian Base Communities in Brazil* (Philadelphia: Temple University Press, 1994); and Daniel R. Miller, ed., *Coming of Age: Protestantism in Contemporary Latin America* (Lanham, Md.: University Press of America, 1994).

4. David E. Dixon, "The New Protestantism in Latin America: Remembering What We Already Know, Testing What We Have Learned," *Comparative Politics* (July 1995): 490.

5. Edward Luttwak, "The Missing Dimension," in *Religion, The Missing Dimension of Statecraft*, ed. Douglas Johnston and Cynthia Sampson (New York: Oxford University Press, 1994), 9.

6. Daniel H. Levine, "Religion and Politics in Comparative and Historical Perspective," *Comparative Politics* 19 (October 1986): 96.

7. A brief sample listing of political science works in English on liberation theology includes Daniel H. Levine, *Popular Voices in Latin American Catholicism* (Princeton, N.J.: Princeton University Press, 1992); Daniel H. Levine, ed., *Religion and Political Conflict in Latin America* (Chapel Hill: University of North Carolina Press, 1986); Scott Mainwaring, *The Catholic Church and Politics in Brazil, 1916–1985* (Stanford, Calif.: Stanford University Press, 1986); Scott Mainwaring and Alexander Wilde, eds., *The Progressive Church in Latin America* (Indiana: University of Notre Dame Press, 1983); Arthur F. McGovern, *Liberation Theology and Its Critics: Toward an Assessment* (Maryknoll, N.Y.: Orbis, 1989); John R. Pottenger, *The Political Theory of Liberation Theology: Toward a Reconvergence of Social Values and Social Science* (Albany: State University of New York Press, 1986); and Paul Sigmund, *Liberation Theology at the Crossroads: Democracy or Revolution?* (New York: Oxford University Press, 1990).

8. Paul E. Sigmund, "Christian Democracy, Liberation Theology, and Political Culture in Latin America," in *Political Culture and Democracy in Developing Countries*, ed. Larry Diamond (Boulder, Colo.: Lynne Rienner, 1993), 329.

9. Stoll, "Introduction," in *Rethinking Protestantism*, 2.

10. Carol Ann Drogus, "The Rise and Decline of Liberation Theology: Churches, Faith, and Political Change in Latin America," *Comparative Politics* (July 1995): 470.

11. It is striking that the bias against the study of the evangelical movement in developing countries is evident within the religious academy as well. As a professor at Yale Divinity School notes, "It's ironic that a divinity school can carry out its mission largely uninterested in Christianity's unprecedented expansion around the world. . . . Perhaps it's a measure of how much we have turned our back on the historical dimension of Christianity and on non-Western societies." Lamin Sanneh, "Global Christianity and the Re-education of the West," *Christian Century*, 19–26 July 1995, 715.

12. Inter-Hemispheric Education Resource Center, "The Rise of the Religious Right in Central America," *Resource Center Bulletin* summer/fall 1987): 4. Also in this vein see Sara Diamond, *Spiritual Warfare: The Politics of the Christian Right* (Boston: South End, 1989), esp. chapters 5, 6, and 7; Ana Maria Ezcurra, *The Neoconservative Offensive: U.S. Churches and Ideological Struggle for Latin America* (New York: New York Circus Publications, 1986); Laura Nuzzi O'Shaughnessy, "Onward Christian Soldiers: The Case of Protestantism in Central America," in *Religious Resurgence and Politics in the Contemporary World*, ed. by Emile Sahliyeh (Albany: State University of New York Press, 1990); and Susan D. Rose and Steve Brouwer, "The

Export of Fundamentalist Americanism: U.S. Evangelical Education in Guatemala," *Latin American Perspectives* (fall 1990): 42–56.

13. Drogus, "Rise and Decline of Liberation Theology," and John Burdick, "Rethinking the Study of Social Movements: The Case of Christian Base Communities in Urban Brazil," in *The Making of Social Movements in Latin America: Identity, Strategy, and Democracy*, ed. Arturo Escobar and Sonia E. Alvarez (Boulder, Colo: Westview, 1992), 171–84.

14. See note 3.

15. Levine, "Religion and Politics in Comparative Historical Perspective," 101.

16. Levine, "Religion and Politics in Comparative Historical Perspective," 99. Levine brings this approach to his own in-depth research of Catholic CEBs in Venezuela and Colombia, which led him to identify tools for empowerment such as lay Bible reading and a theology of a personal relationship with Christ. These are, ironically, the central identifying traits of Protestantism, which Levine does not examine for comparisons. See his *Popular Voices* and "Religious Change, Empowerment and Power: Reflections on Latin American Experience," in *Organized Religion in the Political Transformation of Latin America*, ed. Satya R. Pattnayak (Lanham, Md.: University Press of America, 1995), 15–41.

17. Fernando Calderon, Alejandro Piscitelli, and José Luis Reyna, "Social Movements: Actors, Theories, Expectations," in Escobar and Alvarez, *Social Movements*, 25.

18. For a brilliant theological analysis of how Christianity challenges an oppressive state and inspires movements, see Walter Wink, *Engaging the Powers: Discernment and Resistance in a World of Domination* (Minneapolis: Fortress, 1992).

19. Arturo Escobar, "Culture, Economics, and Politics in Latin American Social Movements Theory and Research," in Escobar and Alvarez, *Social Movements*, 70–71.

20. Sidney Tarrow, *Power in Movement: Social Movements, Collective Action and Politics* (New York: Cambridge University Press, 1994), 3–4.

21. Rhys Williams, "Movement Dynamics and Social Change: Transforming Fundamentalist Ideology and Organizations," in *Accounting for Fundamentalisms: The Dynamic Character of Movements*, ed. Martin E. Marty and R. Scott Appleby (Illinois: University of Chicago Press, 1994), 786.

22. Sonia E. Alvarez and Arturo Escobar, "Conclusion: Theoretical and Political Horizons of Change in Contemporary Latin American Social Movements," in Escobar and Alvarez, *Social Movements*, 322.

23. Escobar, "Culture, Economics and Politics," 68–69.

24. Tarrow, *Power in Movement*, 18.

25. Roy Peterson, Director of External Relations, Summer Institute of Linguistics, interview with author, Guatemala City, Guatemala, 2 November 1993.

26. Christian Lalive d'Epinay, *Haven to the Masses,* and Emilio Willems, *Followers of the New Faith*, are in this tradition. See discussion in Williams, "Movement Dynamics," 788–89. Wuthnow and Lawson prefer "cultural articulation" theory to social movement theory for analyzing religious movements because articulation emphasizes the fit between ideology and surrounding social structure, but not to the degree that the movement's ideologies are subsumed by the social environment. However, we assert that social movement theory can also include such subtle analysis, particularly as presented by Tarrow. See Robert Wuthnow and Matthew P. Lawson, "Sources of Christian Fundamentalism in the United States," in Marty and Appleby, *Accounting for Fundamentalisms*, 18–56.

27. Levine, "Religious Change," 25.

28. Wuthnow and Lawson, "Sources of Christian Fundamentalism," 23–24.

29. "Soul Trafficking," *Latinamerica Press*, 8 February 1996, 6.

Chapter Two

Protestant Missionary Invasion

We avoid the word 'missionary' because it is so often misunderstood.

— Roy Peterson
Director of External Relations
Summer Institute of Linguistics
Guatemala City, 1993

The Summer Institute of Linguistics (SIL) does not sound like an evangelical missionary organization, and this was probably the intent of its founder, William Cameron Townsend. The SIL was incorporated in California in the 1930s as the foreign mission branch of Wycliffe Bible Translators. SIL's link with Protestant missions was obscured by the academic-sounding name, making the organization less offensive to Catholic Latin American governments from the beginning. As illustrated in the opening quotation, the SIL remains sensitive to public relations. Nevertheless, its aggressive proselytizing among indigenous people and its political linkages have made the SIL and Wycliffe Bible Translators perhaps the most controversial mission organization in Latin America (in competition with the notorious New Tribes Mission based in Florida, which works in South America).[1]

Townsend, even posthumously referred to as "Uncle Cam," first worked as a missionary in Guatemala with the Central American Mission, but he was especially drawn to the Mayan people who speak twenty-two different languages and even more dialects. The story goes that he broke away from CAM to form his own organization for translating the Bible after one of the indigenous said to him, "If your God is so big, why doesn't he speak my language?"[2] Thanks to support from the wealthy and the powerful in the United States, (including the Rockefellers), Wycliffe spread around the world and now has over six thousand members. This includes over four hundred doctorate-holding linguists and anthropologists, scholars who apparently are not swayed by the "Enlightenment prejudice" against religion. In Central America approximately eighty SIL employees who work in Guatemala with the indigenous Mayans do not work at all with ladino populations. The controversy that surrounds the SIL is due to Townsend's unabashed ties with Latin American dictators and the U.S. elite, associations of mutual convenience that lasted for decades and have been reported in several sources.[3] Scholars have also pointed out the link between Protestants in Central America in the 1800s and the development of the export-oriented coffee economy. Thus, as Argentine theologian José Míguez Bonino points out, that *original* mingling of U.S. missionary work with capitalist ideology has made it difficult for some Latin American evangelicals to identify with the more progressive, social activist teachings within Protestant theology.[4]

Not only have missionaries been exporters of an economic ideology, they have at times been pawns of specific U.S. foreign policy tactics. The following overview helps to explain how the actions of some U.S. religious and political leaders have contributed to a long-standing disdain for missionaries among progressive observers, a disdain of which the missionaries are well aware. The history of the exploitation of the majority of the people in these countries is long and bloody, and the examples that follow belong to that history. Before we can examine Protestantism as a *movement* in Central America, we must examine the role it has played as a *tool* of propaganda and oppression.

MIXING CHURCH AND STATE

Events in Guatemala in the 1980s illustrate the complex manipulation of religion by politics and the tragic, violent insertion of international foreign policy into village life. Guerrillas in Guatemala have been engaged in a war against the military for well over thirty years, even as peace talks proceed. Instead of engaging in open warfare against the guerrillas, the military in Guatemala has been operating for many years under the principle euphemistically termed "low-intensity conflict." This principle combines development initiatives with intimidation and violent "security" campaigns against guerrilla supporters. Tom Barry and Deborah Preusch, researchers at the Inter-Hemispheric Resource Center in New Mexico, explain how "pacification" and "stabilization" have been integral parts of low-intensity conflict, particularly in Guatemala:

> Pacification usually refers to attempts to control and possibly win over rural communities through the distribution of humanitarian assistance (mainly food, clothes, and medicine) in the context of counterinsurgency conflicts. Pacification is often described as 'winning hearts and minds'. Stabilization is the term AID [the U.S. Agency for International Development] uses for its efforts to prop up economically allied governments in the third world. . . . Neither stabilization nor pacification can rightly be labeled a development strategy. They are strategies to control political and economic crises.[5]

The Reagan administration strongly endorsed the doctrine of low-intensity conflict as a means of supposedly achieving democracy and defeating socialism. The U.S. endorsement became particularly enthusiastic when the military leader in Guatemala also happened to be a born-again Protestant converted by Gospel Outreach missionaries from California. This military officer was General Efraín Ríos Montt. He became the first Protestant president of Guatemala via a 1982 military coup. Evangelicals in the United States were elated at the rise to power of a fellow Protestant in the traditionally Catholic country. Perhaps naively, some evangelical groups became a conduit of aid, serving both the U.S. government and the Guatemalan military.

For instance, conservative religious groups from the U.S. were taken to conflictive areas in Guatemala by army helicopters. Love Lift International, the relief division of Gospel Outreach, delivered supplies designated for military use to the Guatemalan highlands.[6] Members of the Summer Institute of Linguistics conducted humanitarian tasks in the Guatemalan highlands under military direction in the 1980s as part of the campaign to pacify villagers being recruited by guerrillas. The SIL scholars were, in fact, essential to implementing military goals in a country with twenty-two spoken languages. As one such missionary explained, "We knew the language and so we were helicoptered in . . . we were a bridge between the military and the people."[7] Ríos Montt was seen as a "brother in the faith"; never mind the fact that his soldiers were conducting a ruthless "scorched earth" campaign of burning over four hundred villages and killing thousands of suspected counterinsurgents. Survivors of this wave of terrorism, which was most intense in 1982, were then resettled in "model villages" as part of the pacification strategy. Not surprisingly, the missionaries and Ríos Montt insist that reports about terrorism in the early 1980s are false and result from bias among the liberal U.S. news media.[8]

The United States government has also participated in the manipulation of missionaries. Although church and state are more or less separated in domestic politics, the U.S. government has routinely taken sides in religious rivalries to the south for the sake of political goals. For instance, in 1969 Nelson Rockefeller chaired a commission that alerted members of Congress to the changes in the Latin American Catholic Church that could have negative effects on U.S.-Latin American relations. He was referring to the early, reformist rumblings of liberation theology that were politically leftist.[9] The U.S. government response to liberation theology continued in 1983 when Senator Jeremiah Denton of Alabama chaired hearings on the topic of "Marxism and Christianity in Revolutionary Central America," which were staged and publicized to intimidate liberation theologians in the region. A propaganda piece entitled "Persecution of Religious Groups in Nicaragua," published by the White House Office of Media Relations and Planning in 1984 also addressed religion and politics in the region.[10]

As progressives in the Catholic Church lost favor with certain segments of the U.S. government, the evangelical churches gained it. A special briefing was held in 1982 at the U.S. State Department for invited leaders of the Christian Right. In a blatant display of political influence, the government urged religious leaders to mobilize their followers to support Ríos Montt.[11] Advantages adhering to the Christian Right leaders in exchange for their foreign policy cooperation were implicitly, if not explicitly, clear. Pioneer missionary Cameron Townsend after all, had also enjoyed the power, access, and protection that his political contacts had brought him.

United States policy toward El Salvador in the 1980s, like that toward Guatemala, was based on pacification and stabilization. In an effort to support the ruling government and pacify insurgents—and those believed to support them—the U.S. combined economic, humanitarian, and military aid to carry out its low-intensity conflict strategy. The aid was given in the context of a civil war in which the government employed inhumane tactics. For instance, the Salvadoran military conducted a campaign of aerial bombing sporadically in 1984 at the behest of U.S. military advisors. In many areas crops were burned and supplies were cut off in an effort to starve the people and to relocate guerrilla supporters to areas controlled by the military. Once the displacement of guerrilla "supporters" was complete, the remaining population was then aided by the U.S. government.[12] Thus in 1985 El Salvador received $44 million in U.S. food aid, more than any other Latin American country.[13] This can be a very successful tactic. According to one sociologist, "Food aid is not just a pound of beans. It is a pound of beans that generates sympathy to those who distribute it and it gives them credibility in the eyes of the community. Food Aid is power."[14] Much of the aid was distributed through private organizations, primarily religious organizations. The A.I.D. has long recognized churches as efficient vehicles for distributing food aid because they have access to the most remote regions of many countries. However, in El Salvador, Catholic Relief Services (CRS), the Mennonite Central Committee, and the Lutheran Church declined to work with the U.S. A.I.D. because the U.S. was known to have pacifying motives and was the main source of support to one of the warring parties.[15] These humanitarian organizations' refusal to cooperate demonstrates that the cynical, political use of the food assistance was understood. But A.I.D. officials were able to find other religious groups to distribute their goods.

Perhaps the most blatant use of religion for U.S. political purposes occurred in Nicaragua where U.S. policy supported the Nicaraguan contras against the Sandinista government in the 1980s. Following the fall of the Somoza regime in 1979, the Carter administration attempted to pull the Sandinistas toward the United States by immediately calling for $75 million in aid to the new government.[16] With the election of the Ronald Reagan in 1980, however, and the cold war division of the world into camps of good and evil, the young Sandinista government was designated an enemy of the United States, and by 1982 all U.S. aid had been terminated.[17]

Whereas U.S. policy toward other Central American nations centered around stabilization during the Reagan years, the policy goal in regard to Nicaragua was clearly destabilization of the economy and the ruling Sandinista government. As the U.S. terminated its assistance to Nicaragua and carried out its destabilization plan, it concurrently increased aid to Nicaragua's neighbors, Costa Rica and Honduras to enlist their help in its war against the Sandinistas. The facts regarding the U.S.-led counterinsurgency in Nicaragua are well documented.[18] But where do evangelicals fit into the scenario?

While the U.S. was helping organize the contras near the Honduran and Nicaraguan borders, many conservative U.S. evangelical groups were beginning to operate in the area. The most prominent of these were Pat Robertson's 700 Club, Jimmy Swaggart's Missions in Motion and the Christian Emergency Relief Teams (CERT). In just one example, in 1985 Swaggart flew over a Miskito Indian refugee camp in Honduras dropping candy from his plane for children while his message about Christ and Communism boomed throughout the area.[19] Back in the United States a propaganda war was also being waged on the American people. Lieutenant Colonel Oliver North of the U.S. National Security Council staff was a central player in this extensive campaign among U.S. evangelical missionaries and sympathizers to build a private support network for the contras, a campaign that was reviewed during U.S. Senate investigative hearings.[20] Pat Robertson raised money by preaching against the evils of Marxism on his Christian Broadcast Network, claiming that the contras were "God's army." David Courson of CERT stated in his money-raising efforts that the "Sandinistas are determined to eliminate all Christians. . . . Thousands of people have been brutally murdered because they would neither deny Christ nor submit to the brutal demands of the Sandinistas."[21] Various provocative fundraising activities agreed with White House policy seeking to weaken the Sandinista government, and they were part of the effort to undermine the Boland Amendment passed by the U.S. Congress prohibiting military aid to the contras at the time.

By no means, however, were all evangelical organizations working in concert with U.S. attempts to undermine Sandinista rule, a
point we will examine further in chapter 5. The Moravian Church
provides us with an example of how the U.S. government worked
against an organization's efforts to bring peace to the war torn
nation. The Moravian Church had been part of the Miskito Indian community on the Atlantic coast of Nicaragua since the nine-
teenth century when it was introduced by German missionaries.
In the 1980s the Miskito's attempts at autonomy resulted in a brief
war with the Sandinistas, and many Moravian pastors fled with
exiles to Honduras and even helped to lead an armed insurrec-
tion. Later, however, the Moravians and Baptists mediated peace
talks between the Sandinistas and Yatama—the indigenous organization. These peace efforts, however, were not well-received by
the U.S. government. According to Gerald Skhlabach, a Mennonite worker in Nicaragua, a U.S. State Department official con-
fessed to a Miskito church leader that the U.S. did not want the
Miskito situation to go away because it was the best case against
the Sandinistas.[22] The CIA also appears to have tried to remove
Moravians from the peace process. In December 1987 a plot was
uncovered to assassinate Lutheran pastor Ulrich Epperlein and
Moravian pastors John Paul Lederach and Higgins Miller in an
effort to remove them from the peace process.[23] The Baptist minister involved in the mediation, when asked about the U.S. involvement, simply responded, "We were persecuted by the C.I.A."[24]
The Moravian example illustrates that in its war against the Sandinistas the U.S. was willing to work actively against evangelical
efforts to resolve the conflict, even as it used evangelicals to further the contra cause.

Given government manipulation of missionaries in Central
America, it is not surprising that observers have been suspicious
of their motives and goals. But as we shall see, the evangelical
missionaries are not cut from one cloth. Many have worked for
social reforms and even revolutionary ends, just as many have
opposed or ignored reformist policies.

Many evangelical missionaries are motivated by purely religious
goals, but they are not educated about the cultural or political
setting of the receiving countries. It may be difficult for more
cynical observers to accept that the missionaries generally do not

have specific political objectives, but while attending a large missionary school in Costa Rica, I became convinced that the majority of these missionary novices were politically naive. The students eagerly participated in inspirational worship services, but few attended the lectures by historians and anthropologists. Many were extremely uninformed about hemispheric politics, although they were experts in quoting Scripture. A fascinating recent study of missionaries as sociological "strangers" raises the point that missionaries are often as estranged from their homeland's culture and political ideology as they are from that of their host country, and that they form supportive but isolated enclaves with other missionaries.[25] One result of the lack of knowledge about politics and about the societies they are ostensibly serving is that these missionaries are susceptible to manipulation by the governments of North and Central America. They may even be subjected to manipulation by some of their own organizational leaders who have political agendas that are not widely understood by the missionary troops. The visiting professor in Costa Rica complained about how mission agencies send out uninformed evangelists. It is easy for field missionaries to become pawns in political power struggles. "It may be innocent when missionaries become involved in such politics," he said, "but it's an innocence that's culpable."[26]

The contributions that some missionaries have made to military objectives, economic oppression, and human rights violations have brought shame to mission work. Nevertheless, the *long-term impact* of the cynical use of missionaries described above should not be exaggerated. Evangelical church members in Central America are not passive objects who incorporate the ideology of North Americans passing through. It is ludicrous to think that Jimmy Swaggart's sermon, shouted from a candy-dropping helicopter, had much effect on the campesinos other than providing brief entertainment. Blatant U.S. government manipulation of the missionaries has damaged the missionaries' credibility, but these often crude interventions have not significantly impacted Central America. The long-term, committed evangelicals and the now nationalized churches they encouraged are the sources of the movement. Thus, analysts should avoid focus on the dramatic episodes described above and study the goals, practices, and ideologies of Central American evangelicals.

For example, many evangelical churches in the region have provided valuable assistance to neighborhood programs that mobilize people rather than pacify them. An *Asambleas de Dios* preacher works also as a labor leader for electrical workers in Guatemala. He described to me the efforts of some evangelical organizations in the spring of 1989 calling for a just wage in Guatemala, which only resulted in harassment and intimidation from the government and the bombing of one church.[27] Even during the Ríos Montt presidency in 1982 Protestants were not immune from terrorism. In El Quiché, thirty members of a Pentecostal church were killed while at worship because they were suspected of radicalism.[28] The indiscriminate attacks continue. Presbyterian human rights workers Manuel Saquic and Pascual Serech were murdered in 1995 in Guatemala, and their co-workers at the Maya Kakchiquel Presbytery received death threats.[29] Terrorism continues in Nicaragua as well. For example, in July 1995 rearmed contra groups ("recontras") attacked members of the United Pentecostal Church who were on their way to celebrate the sixteenth anniversary of the Sandinista revolution.[30]

The evangelicals are not a monolithic, conservative mass bound to the status quo. Rather, they are autonomous and their political orientations depend on the local context. They may elect to join protest movements or they may attempt to remain apolitical, providing safe haven for members seeking refuge from violence, if that is what is needed at the moment. The social advantage of taking an apolitical position is that the churches may then engage in needed aid distribution programs without provoking counterinsurgency terrorism that would shut them down.[31] This is certainly not a revolutionary approach, but it *is* pragmatic and humanitarian. In either case the active evangelical laity often includes religious freethinkers who resist control by U.S. founding missions or by U.S. government agencies. It is difficult—but not impossible—for U.S. citizens to hold the U.S. government accountable for a foreign policy that uses religious networks such as the ones we have described here because the use is often covert and requires investigative research. There is a certain poetic justice, however, in the fact that weak accountability is a double-edged sword that can work against progressive or conservative policies. Recipients of aid in such a decentralized, autonomous system can be more assertive, more reactionary, more radical, and more independent than predicted. Ultimately the political direction that individual churches take is up to them.

In a deeper theological sense we need to remember that the local context shapes not only the religious and political activities but the teachings of the pastors and the overall Protestant message as well. Again, the people are not simply objects absorbing a prepackaged delivery but are actively reforming a theology even as they respond. Protestant scholar Andrew Walls provides perspective on the significance of the movement *for the development of Christianity*:

> Within a very short period of time the conditions which have produced the phenomena characteristic of Christianity for almost a millennium have largely disappeared. After centuries in which the norms by which Christian expression have been tested have arisen from the history and conditions of the Mediterranean world and of the lands north and east of it, the process has been transferred into a new and infinitely more varied theatre of activity. The conditions of African and Melanesian life, the intellectual climate of India, the political battlegrounds of Latin America, increasingly provide the context within which the Christian mind is being formed. The process is already beginning to produce changes in Christian priorities, and in the structure of Christian thought, practice and government. Indeed, most of the discernible changes in Christianity since 1945 come from this fundamental southward shift.[32]

In chapters 3 and 4 we will return to this important theme as we examine the ongoing evolution of religious priorities and practice in Central America.

If political direction, ideology, and theology were simply imposed by North American missionaries, then Protestantism in Central America would lack the autonomy so essential to forming an authentic collective identity. In the 1990s the evidence is strong that local churches have found their autonomy from the North American religious\political right. They lead their own churches, form their own umbrella organizations, practice their own theology, and will soon send out more missionaries than they receive.[33] The focus on missionaries to Central America in the 1980s by U.S. politicians and interest groups combating "communism" was obsessive and extreme. It is not surprising that most evangelicals in the region are now eager to sever their ties with North American politicians and move on, as we will do after one more back-ward glance.

EVANGELICAL MISSIONARY PATTERNS

An understanding of the ramifications of evangelicalism in Cen-tral America must begin with at least an overview of the modest beginnings of Protestantism.[34] A coordinated plan by North Ameri-can Protestants, infamous for its cultural callousness, was formu-lated at a meeting in 1916 referred to as the "Congress of Panama." The U.S. mission boards of the larger Protestant de-nominations set the agenda for the meeting, which was attended by only twenty-one native Latin Americans out of 304 partici-pants. English was the official language of the conference.[35] The denominations entered into "comity agreements" that divided Lat-in America into regions for evangelism by the different church organizations in order to avoid duplication of effort. El Salvador, Honduras, and Nicaragua were assigned to the American (North-ern) Baptists. The Methodists focused on Panama and Costa Rica and the Presbyterians laid claim to Guatemala. These denomina-tions, along with a few other long-established denominations, are now labeled the "historic" Protestant churches. In spite of the careful mission strategizing that occurred at the Congress of Pan-ama, it must be concluded that these mainline denominations made only modest progress in converting Latin American Catholics—especially in light of what was to come.

"Faith missions" comprised another missionary wave in the early 1900s that was roughly parallel to the evangelism of the historic churches but had a more conservative theology. The founding fa-ther of the faith missions was the famous fundamentalist preach-er, Cyrus Ingerson Scofield who founded the Central American Mission (CAM) in 1890.[36] Over the years CAM has constructed hundreds of churches and has sponsored schools, medical clinics, day care centers, and distribution of surplus food received from U.S. A.I.D. It also owns radio stations and oversees the Guate-mala Bible Institute and the Central America Theological Semi-nary. It is a major force in the evangelical movement throughout Central America.[37] The most well-known offspring of CAM was William Cameron Townsend, who was introduced at the beginning of the chapter. Another prominent mission organization, the Latin American Evangelization Campaign (later, the Latin America Mission), formed during the early twentieth century. It works among the poor in the region, primarily in the cities.

The distinguishing trait of faith missions is that they are nondenominational. Each missionary must find sponsorship from friends and various churches back home, not from a denominational headquarters. For instance, the SIL workers solicit their own financial support from numerous churches and give the first 10 percent to "Uncle Cam," i.e., the organization. This is significant because although most missionary organizations may have an official theological statement, the loose financial structure means that the missionaries actually have great autonomy in the theology that they preach and in the types of local churches that they encourage. Despite meager funding this flexible grassroots approach has allowed faith missions to penetrate Central America and to spread more quickly than the historic churches with strong denominational ties. They can provide religious goods and services at a lower marginal cost than either Catholic parishes or the historic Protestants.[38] As one study of Pentecostal churches in El Salvador notes, "[d]ecentralization does not threaten the growth of Protestantism, nor do church schisms. Indeed, Protestantism grows by schism and decentralization."[39]

The faith missions do not require rigorous theological training, as do the more bureaucratized historic churches and the Catholic Church—years of training are required for Catholic priests and nuns. Extensive scholarly training has not been essential for most evangelicals, as was noted previously. They have emphasized outreach training instead. For example, during the 1960s the LAM coordinated evangelism-in-depth campaigns in ten countries, involving numerous evangelical denominations in mobilization training, radio outreach, nightly meetings, and evangelical parades—not in theological study.[40]

The Assemblies of God denomination deserves special mention because it is the largest evangelical church in El Salvador, Guatemala, and Nicaragua, as well as being very strong in Honduras. It could be called the wellspring of the powerful Pentecostal branch of Protestantism. Like all Protestant groups, it began as an imported missionary church. Now, after sixty years, it is thoroughly nationalized in each Central American country. It is associated with thousands of individual churches across Central America, mostly in poor rural areas, but the precise number is virtually impossible to ascertain because the churches may start up in any available site without any official registration. The Assemblies of God organization runs dozens of primary schools, Bible schools, clinics, and service centers throughout the region. They are largely financed by Jimmy Swaggart Ministries based in Missouri, although the churches themselves are self-supporting. In Guatemala, for instance, Assemblies of God run fifteen schools and five seminaries; in El Salvador the church directs its own university, thirty primary schools, and four Bible schools.[41] Swaggart is still the most famous Assemblies of God leader, gaining popularity through his broadcasts, crusades, and revivals. However, sex scandals that were publicized in 1985 have caused him to be largely discredited. Ironically, Swaggart's disgrace has probably accelerated the growth rate of the churches because they became even more independent of the U.S. organization, relying on indigenous pastors and administrators rather than on foreign missionaries. The national superintendent of the *Asambleas de Dios en Guatemala* was adamant during an interview about the complete independence of his church from Jimmy Swaggart and the United States.[42]

Table 2.1 lists the eight largest evangelical groups in each of the five countries, in terms of their long-term missionary personnel (far more U.S. evangelicals visit for brief periods). This listing indicates both the diversity of U.S. mission groups working in Central America and the ones that have become most established, particularly the Central American Mission and the Assemblies of God Foreign Mission.

When we look comparatively at the nations of Central America, as in Table 2.2, we see considerable variation in the missionary focus among the five neighboring countries—despite the overarching patterns described above. What variables account for this variation? One unpredictable factor that influences the number of missionaries is the occurrence of natural disasters, to which religious organizations invariably respond with additional personnel and aid. Cynics would say that the missionaries come to recruit the people when they are grateful for assistance and more vulnerable to religious persuasion; other observers say the height-

Chapter Two

Table 2.1
Eight Largest U.S. Evangelical Organizations in
Selected Central American Nations, Listed by Number
of Long-Term U.S. Personnel, 1992

Costa Rica

Number of Personnel	Mission	Year of Founding
68	Latin America Mission	1921
32	Southern Baptist Foreign Mission	1949
26	Central American Mission Int'l.	1891
22	Calvary International	1982
24	Assemblies of God Foreign Mission	1936
17	Christian Reformed World Missions	1982
15	Baptist Bible Fellowship Int'l.	1968
14	Churches of Christ	1967

El Salvador

Number of Personnel	Mission	Year of Founding
25	Assemblies of God Foreign Mission	1925
9	Harvesting in Spanish	1977
8	Mennonite Central Committee	1981
5	Southern Baptist Foreign Mission	1975
4	Adib Eden Evangelical Missionary Soc.	1968
4	Central American Mission Int'l.	1896
4	United Pentecostal Church Int'l.	1975
4	Youth With A Mission	1984

Guatemala

Number of Personnel	Mission	Year of Founding
47	Living Water Teaching Int'l.	1979
50	Southern Baptist Foreign Mission	1948
50	Central American Mission Int'l.	1899
24	Assemblies of God Foreign Mission	1916
18	Overseas Crusade Int'l., Inc.	1979
18	Calvary International	1987
18	Globe Missionary Evangelism	1980
17	Church of the Nazarene World Mission	?
16	Habitat for Humanity Internat'l.	1979

Honduras

Number of Personnel	Mission	Year of Founding
40	Southern Baptist Foreign Mission	1954
37	World Gospel Mission	1944
17	Assemblies of God Foreign Mission	1942

17	Central American Mission Int'l.	1896
13	Mission Aviation Fellowship	1952
12	Baptist International Missions	1970
10	Brethren Assemblies	?
10	Christian Reformed World Missions	1971
10	Church of God World Missions	1944

Nicaragua

Number of Personnel	Mission	Year of Founding
13	Habitat for Humanity Int'l.	1984
13	Mennonite Central Committee	1979
12	Presbyterian Church USA	?
11	United Methodist Church	?
7	American Baptist Churches USA	1917
6	Southern Baptist Foreign Mission	?
4	Calvary International	1990
3	Young Life	1988

Source: Compiled from *Mission Handbook*, 15th ed. (Monrovia, Calif.: Mission Advanced Research Center, 1993), pp. 291–418.

ened presence of missionaries following disasters is a humanitarian response that only coincidentally results in Protestant conversions. In Guatemala the disaster factor was most evident after the horrific 1976 earthquake that killed over twenty thousand persons. In Honduras Hurricane Fifi in 1974 brought a new wave of evangelical missionaries.[43] A very similar effect occurred after the 1972 earthquake in Nicaragua. The inter-denominational organization called CEPAD (*Comité Evangélico Pro Ayuda de los Damnificados*), since renamed the *Comité Evangélico Pro Ayuda al Desarrollo*), was formed four days after the earthquake when Gustavo Parajon issued a radio appeal to Protestant pastors to coordinate their relief efforts. Twenty denominations responded, and five different aid programs were formed within three weeks.[44] As we shall see in chapter 5, CEPAD remains an active, highly respected Protestant organization known throughout the country.

Several minor factors are also involved in the varied U.S. mission presence in the region. Costa Rica has more missionaries than any country in the region (except Guatemala), yet it has a smaller population and has experienced fewer of the natural and political/economic disasters that have plagued the rest of the region. The primary reason for the large number of U.S. Protestant mis-

Table 2.2
Number of Long-Term U.S. Protestant Missionaries
in Five Central American Nations, 1992

Country	No. of Missionaries	Missionary/Population
Costa Rica	362	1/8,803
Honduras	320	1/15,468
Guatemala	430	1/22,756
Nicaragua	95	1/40,832
El Salvador	87	1/64,080

Source: Compiled from *Mission Handbook*, 15th ed. (Monrovia, Calif.: Mission Advanced Research Center, 1993), pp. 292-414.

sionaries in Costa Rica is institutional. This small, stable nation serves as a training ground for mission students about to depart throughout Latin America. For instance, the *Seminario Bíblico Latinoamericano* is located there, as is a regional office for the Latin American Mission (LAM), the *Escuela de Estudios Pastorales* (School for Pastoral Studies), and the *Instituto de Lengua Española*, a large Spanish language school that caters to Protestant missionaries.

These missionaries are not necessarily concentrated where one might rationally expect them to be, i.e., where the number of "unchurched" people is greatest. For instance, World Vision recently chided the rest of the missionary community for the fact that only 1.2 percent of foreign mission funding is designated to the "least-evangelized world," i.e., North Africa, the Middle East, and the Far East.[45] But "faith missionaries" freely choose the country in which they wish to do evangelistic work. Gustavo Parajon of Nicaragua hypothesized—only half facetiously—that as few as one hundred Protestant missionaries now work in Nicaragua because it is the hottest, most humid of the Central American nations; the more temperate Guatemala has over four hundred such missionaries.[46]

The most important factor behind the varied presence of U.S. missionaries, probably, is the political dynamic with which we began this chapter. This has been the case since the beginning of the Protestant movement in Central America. For instance, in the late 1800s a few liberal, modernizing governments sought to counter conservative Catholic dominance by instilling Protestantism. Thus, in 1882 President Justo Rufino Barrios brought Presbyterian missionary John Clark Hill from the U.S. to Guatemala with the long-term goal of weakening the political power of the Catholic Church. Barrios was a liberal dictator who was decidedly anticlerical. He deeded the Presbyterians land for their church that was situated across from the Roman Catholic cathedral in Guatemala City. Similarly, President José Santos Zelaya of Nicaragua invited Protestant missionaries to his country in 1893.[47] These invitations overlapped neatly with U.S. political ambition to have more influence in the region.

We have already observed that Central America became the particular focus of U.S. missionary efforts in the 1980s for political reasons. A missionary wave to Central America occurred throughout the 1980s as the new religious right brand of Protestantism was experiencing an upsurge in the United States that translated into more missionary resources for the south. Rios Montt's coup d'etat in Guatemala in 1982 received enthusiastic support from many Protestants in the States. Similarly, politics had religious implications even for Honduras, which still has a large number of U.S. missionaries per capita. After the Sandinista victory in 1979 the political setting in Nicaragua was unfriendly toward many U.S. evangelicals who had been recruited with a political agenda; therefore, some persistent missionaries stationed themselves in Honduras and worked in border areas with Nicaraguan refugees. On the other hand, missionaries from some mainline denominations were welcomed to work in Nicaragua after the revolution, as we will see in chapter 5. Now let us examine the effectiveness of these missionary resources in Central America, at least in terms of conversion rates.

THE NUMBERS GAME

Just how successful have the evangelicals been in breaking up the ancient Catholic dominance? Before we assess possible political ramifications of Protestantism in the region, we need to get a handle on the scope of the movement. Although conversion rates are supplied in virtually every article and book on the topic, the sources for these figures are problematic.

In 1979 an organization based in California called OC Ministries (formerly Overseas Crusade) came to Guatemala and formed an interdenominational mission organization called *Servicio Evangelizador Para América Latina* (SEPAL). Similar SEPAL offices exist in Brazil, Colombia, Mexico, and Argentina. The role of SEPAL is to train pastors and missionaries in outreach, conduct research, and assist Protestants in setting up Sunday schools at the grassroots level. SEPAL sponsored a motivational evangelical campaign called "Mission 90" which set the ambitious goal of converting 50 percent of Guatemalans to Protestantism by 1990. Cliff Holland, an evangelical church growth expert, observed that in a Guatemalan government census five times as many people called themselves non-Catholic Christians as were reported on the official Protestant church rolls. Thus, Holland concluded that the number of evangelicals in Guatemala was approximately the number of evangelical church memberships multiplied by four (in order to leave out quasi-Christian groups such as Mormons and Jehovah's Witness). This virtually arbitrary estimation is the source of the frequently cited figure of 22.4 percent evangelicals within the Guatemalan population in 1982.[48] Similarly shaky survey results quoted by SEPAL in 1987 found 31.6 percent of the Guatemalan population to be evangelical.[49] Obviously SEPAL had a vested interest in inflating the figures in order to sustain the enthusiasm and fundraising power of "Mission 90." They eagerly report figures that use "multiplier effects" of three or four to account for extraneous factors, but they do not use a similar reverse process to account for evangelical dropouts.

Patrick Johnstone is a missiologist who has published more recent estimates of evangelical church growth in Central America, which allow some comparisons of estimates within the region.

Another estimate claimed that the number of evangelicals in all of Latin America doubled to over fifty million during the 1980s.[50] Brazil and Chile, which account for 40 percent of the Latin American population, have both experienced phenomenal rates of conversion. But again the estimates are extremely rough, especially when they are extrapolated into future decades by merely assuming constant rates of conversion, as in Johnstone's Table 2.3.

TABLE 2.3
Percent Protestant Estimates for Selected
Central American Nations, 1993

Country	1993 Estimated Percent Protestant	Estimated time to double at current growth rates
Costa Rica	11	8 years
El Salvador	21	12 years
Guatemala	24	8 years
Honduras	11	12 years
Nicaragua	17	9 years

Source: Patrick Johnstone, *Operation World* (Grand Rapids, Mich.: Zondervan, 1993).

Protestant growth has slowed considerably in Chile but continues elsewhere; growth is a variable process.

Protestantism throughout Latin America is highly fluid, and most of the data surrounding the movement has been disseminated with false authority. On the one hand, Protestant missionary organizations have a bias to report dramatic conversion rates. On the other hand, some of the recent critics of the inflationary nature of the figures are Catholic and have a bias toward deriding the rival religion. For example, despite the obvious explosion of Protestantism, Cardinal Obando y Bravo of Nicaragua made valiant attempts in public to downplay Protestantism. He was quoted in a magazine article a few years ago as estimating that only 1 percent of Nicaraguans were Protestant.[51] For most Latin American nations we do not have even a reliable sample for measurement to know if the estimates are too low or too high. Social scientists are now attempting to conduct more accurate surveys of religious affiliation, but this is extremely difficult in developing nations. Many denominational offices, for instance, do not even have an accurate count of the number of *churches*, much less members.[52] It seems that the most reasonable approach to assessing the Protestant movement in the region is twofold: (1) Be cautious in citing figures of conversion, "considering the source," and (2) do not ignore simple observation in the field that indicates the amazing prevalence of Protestantism. In much of Central America at least evangelical churches now appear in virtually every village and every city neighborhood.

The external intervention of North American missionaries into the culture and society of Central American nations, at times in tandem with the U.S. government, has often been heavy-handed and exploitative. If the background recounted in this chapter were the end of the story, we would not be analyzing a social movement at all, but a clear case of cultural imperialism. However, it is the response of Central Americans to Protestantism as actors, not subjects, that requires closer analysis.

Tarrow argues that powerful movements arise when opportunities are widening, realignments are occurring, and elites are divided.[53] All of these characteristics are true of Central American nations in the mid-1980s and 1990s. Clearly government elites are divided. For instance, the Sandinistas in Nicaragua are internally divided, as are their opponents; as El Salvador struggles with peace, the FMLN revolutionary party met a surprising defeat in the last elections; even the military in Guatemala is openly split into moderate and hard-line factions. Furthermore, the traditionally monolithic Catholic Church appears split into progressive and traditional groupings, as well as other varieties such as the newer charismatic Catholics. Amid the shifts and confusion people are finding allies and common purpose in the array of evangelical churches. Missionaries and U.S. government manipulators do not create a movement. Rather, widening opportunities in the political culture, popular autonomy, and framing symbols that resonate with the people are the source of movement formation. In the next chapter we will examine the movement resources of Protestantism, i.e., the cultural and theological frames that mobilize consensus in this evolving phenomenon.

NOTES

1. See, for example, the exposé by British author Norman Lewis, *The Missionaries* (New York: McGraw-Hill, 1988).

2. Roy Peterson, Director of External Relations, Summer Institute of Linguistics (Guatemala Branch of Wycliffe Bible Translators), interview with author, Guatemala City, 2 November 1993.

3. See exposés by David Stoll, *Fishers of Men or Founders of Empire?* (London: Zed Press; Cambridge, Mass.: Cultural Survival,

1982) and Gerard Colby with Charlotte Dennett, *Thy Will Be Done: The Conquest of the Amazon: Nelson Rockefeller and Evangelism in the Age of Oil* (New York: HarperCollins Publishers, 1995).

4. José Míguez Bonino, Carmelo Alvarez, and Roberto Craig, *Protestantismo y Liberalismo en América Latina*, 2d ed. (San José, Costa Rica: Departmento Ecumenico de Investigaciónes, 1985).

5. Tom Barry and Deborah Preusch, *The Soft War: The Uses and Abuses of U.S. Economic Aid in Central America* (New York: Grove, 1988), 18–19.

6. Barry and Preusch, *Soft War*, 133–34; Sara Diamond, *Spiritual Warfare: The Politics of the Christian Right* (Boston: South End, 1989), 164–68.

7. Inter-Hemispheric Education Resource Center, *Private Organizations with U.S. Connections—Guatemala: Directory and Analysis* (Albuquerque: Inter-Hemispheric Education Resource Center, 1988), 61–62.

8. Author's interview with Gen. Efraín Ríos Montt, Guatemala City, 14 July 1990, in which he discounted the international press as strongly related to the communists. Roy Peterson of the Summer Institute of Linguistics stated, "Ríos Montt is a man of integrity, a true believer. He didn't do all those murders they said," Guatemala City, 2 November 1993.

9. David Stoll, *Is Latin America Turning Protestant? The Politics of Evangelical Growth* (Berkeley: University of California Press, 1990), 34.

10. U.S. Senate, 98th Congress, 1st S., Hearings before the Subcommittee on Security and Terrorism of the Committee on the Judiciary, "Marxism and Christianity in Revolutionary Central America," October 18–19, 1983. Also see Peter Rosset and John Vandermeer, eds., *Nicaragua: Unfinished Revolution* (New York: Grove, 1986), 433–53.

11. Resource Center, *Directory*, 7.

12. Barry and Preusch, *Soft War*, 171–72.

13. Rachel Garst and Tom Barry, *Feeding the Crisis: U.S. Food Aid and Farm Policy in Central America* (Lincoln: University of Nebraska Press, 1990), 12 and 205.

14. Inter-Hemispheric Education Resource Center, "The Rise of the Religious Right in Central America," *Resource Center Bulletin* (summer/fall 1987): 4.

15. Barry and Preusch, *Soft War*, 175–76. Also see "No Arms for El Salvador," *The Christian Century*, 5 April 1989, 346.

16. Barry and Preusch, *Soft War*, 200.

17. Barry and Preusch, *Soft War*, 203.

18. For example, Bradford E. Burns, *At War in Nicaragua: The*

Reagan Doctrine and the Politics of Nostalgia (New York: Harper and Row, 1987); Leslie Cockburn, *Out of Control: The Story of the Reagan Administration's Secret War in Nicaragua, the Illegal Arms Pipeline, and the Contra Drug Connection* (New York: Atlantic Monthly Press, 1987); Morris H. Morley, *Washington, Somoza and the Sandinistas* (New York: Cambridge University Press, 1994); Morris H. Morley, *The Reagan Administration and Nicaragua: How Washington Constructs its Case for Counterrevolution in Central America* (New York: Institute for Media Analysis, 1987); Holly Sklar, *Washington's War on Nicaragua* (Boston: South End, 1988); William I. Robinson, *David and Goliath: The U.S. War Against Nicaragua* (New York: Monthly Review Press, 1987); and Thomas W. Walker, *Reagan versus the Sandinistas: The Undeclared War on Nicaragua* (Boulder, Colo.: Westview, 1987).

19. Barry and Preusch, *Soft War*, 225.

20. The President's Special Review Board, *The Tower Commission Report* (New York: Bantam/Time Books, 1987).

21. Barry and Preusch, *Soft War*, 225.

22. Gerald Schlabach, "Case Study: Nicaragua," *Mennonite Quarterly*, 368–77; Bruce Nichols, "Religious Conciliation between the Sandinistas and the East Coast Indians of Nicaragua," in *Religion, The Missing Dimension of Statecraft*, Douglas Johnston and Cynthia Sampson, eds. (New York: Oxford University Press, 1994), 64–87.

23. Martha Honey and Tony Avirgan, "The CIA's War," *Nation*, 6 February 1988, 155.

24. Gustavo Adolfo Parajon, Executive Director, Comite Evangelico Pro-Ayuda Al Desarrollo (CEPAD), interview with author, Managua, Nicaragua, 12 November 1993.

25. Jeffrey Swanson, *Echoes of the Call: Identity and Ideology among American Missionaries in Ecuador* (New York: Oxford University Press, 1995).

26. John Hall, Professor of Religious Studies, Nazarene Seminario, interview with author, San Jose, Costa Rica, 8 July 1993.

27. Representative from Guatemalan union for electrical workers, STINDE, interview with author, Washington, D.C., 8 June 1990.

28. Martin, *Tongues of Fire*, 254.

29. "Death Threats," *Latinamerica Press*, 24 August 1995, 8; and "Guatemala Officials Promise to Jail Alleged Killer," *The News of the Presbyterian Church (U.S.A.)*, December 1995, 1.

30. "Nicaragua: Recontras Attack July 19 Caravan," *El Diario-La Prensa*, 20 July 1995.

31. Martin, *Tongues of Fire*, 267–68.

32. Andrew Walls, "The Christian Tradition in Today's World," in *Religion in Today's World*, ed. Frank Whaling.

33. John A. Siewert and John A. Kenyon, eds., *Mission Handbook: 1993–95* (Monrovia, Calif.: Mission Advanced Research Center, World-Vision International, 1993), 13.

34. See Carmelo Alvarez, ed., *Pentecostalismo y Liberacion: Una experiencia latinoamericana* (San José, Costa Rica: Departamento Ecumenico de Investigaciónes, 1992), esp. chapter 5; for a useful summary see Roger S. Greenway, "Protestant Missionary Activity in Latin America," in *Coming of Age: Protestantism in Contemporary Latin America*, ed. Daniel R. Miller (Lanham, Md.: University Press of America, 1994), 65–88.

35. Michael Dodson and Laura Nuzzi O'Shaughnessy, *Nicaragua's Other Revolution: Religious Faith and Political Struggle* (Chapel Hill: University of North Carolina Press, 1990), 81.

36. Mike Berg and Paul Pretiz, *The Gospel People* (Monrovia, Calif.: WorldVision International/Latin America Mission, 1992), 47.

37. The Inter-Hemispheric Education Resource Center, *Private Organizations with U.S. Connections—Guatemala: Directory and Analysis*, 29–30; *Private Organizations with U.S. Connections—Honduras: Directory and Analysis*, 31.

38. My thanks to an anonymous reviewer for the distinction that the fairly low start-up cost of the Pentecostal mission is actually true for virtually all religious groups, but is less important than marginal costs, i.e., those costs for forming each additional congregation, which are high for Catholics and inconsequential for Pentecostal churches. Also see Anthony Gill, "The Institutional Limits of Catholic Progressivism: An Economic Approach," *International Journal of Social Economics*, vol. 22 (forthcoming).

39. Kenneth M. Coleman et al., "Protestantism in El Salvador: Conventional Wisdom versus the Survey Evidence," in *Rethinking Protestantism in Latin America*, eds. Virginia Garrard-Burnett and David Stoll (Philadelphia: Temple University Press, 1993), 118.

40. Berg and Pretiz, *Gospel People*, 73, 75.

41. Resource Center, *Guatemala: Directory*, 22.

42. Superintendent, Concilio Nacional de la Asambleas de Dios en Guatemala, interview with author, Guatemala City, 8 July 1990.

43. Resource Center, *Honduras: Directory*, 8.

44. Gustavo Adolfo Parajon, Executive Director, Comité Evangélico ProAyuda Al Desarrollo (CEPAD), interview with author, Managua, Nicaragua, 12 November 1993.

45. John A. Siewert and John A. Kenyon, eds., *Mission Handbook:*

1993–1995 (Monrovia, Calif.: Mission Advanced Research Center, WorldVision International, 1993), 26.

46. Author's interview with Parajon.

47. Roberto Zub Kurylowicz, *Protestantismo y Elecciones en Nicaragua* (Managua, Nicaragua: Centro InterEclesial de Estudios Teologicos y Sociales, 1993), 19.

48. David Stoll, *Is Latin American Turning Protestant? The Politics of Evangelical Growth* (Berkeley: University of California Press, 1990), 125.

49. Resource Center, *Guatemala: Directory*, 7.

50. Laura Nuzzi O'Shaughnessy, "Onward Christian Soldiers: The Case of Protestantism in Central America," in *Religious Resurgence and Politics in the Contemporary World*, ed. Emile Sahliyeh (Albany: State University of New York Press, 1990), 104.

51. Benjamin Cortes, Secretary General, *Central InterEclesial de Estudios Teológicos y Sociales* (CIEETS), interview with author, Managua, Nicaragua, 12 November 1993.

52. Author's interview with Superintendent, *Concilio Nacional de La Asambleas de Dios en Guatemala*. This official estimated that three hundred new churches in his Assemblies of God denomination were founded every year, often without reporting any official notification.

53. Sidney Tarrow, *Power in Movement: Social Movements, Collective Action and Politics* (New York: Cambridge University Press, 1994), 18.

Chapter Three

Who Are They?
Movement Resources

> Evangelical theology in Latin America is being developed. It's a blend of Protestant liberation theology plus Catholic liberation theology plus evangelical theology—plus the Nicaraguan thesis.
>
> — Benjamín Cortés, Secretary General
> Centro InterEclesial de Estudios
> Teológicos y Sociales (CIEETS),
> Managua, Nicarauga, 1993

At this point it is important to explain some religious terminology and theology as it applies to Central America. Again, the term "evangelical" is being used interchangeably with the term "Protestant," in accordance with its usage there. Either word refers to all non-Catholic Christians, including Pentecostals, Fundamentalists, and mainline traditional Protestants, but the quasi-Christian groups such as Jehovah's Witnesses and Mormons, which have very distinctive theologies and are in fact heretical to many evangelicals. The choice of theology and cultural symbols is part of the process of the "framing" of Protestantism as a movement. As sociologist David Snow et al. describe this concept,

> By rendering events or occurrences meaningful, frames function to organize experience and guide action, whether individual or collective. So conceptualized, it follows that frame alignment is a necessary condition for movement participation, whatever its nature or intensity.[1]

Recurring theological themes are what render "events or occurrences meaningful" for the evangelicals, yet as the opening quotation indicates, theology in the region is still being developed and is a hybrid (although the particular hybrid he describes is in a

43

postrevolutionary Nicaraguan context). Throughout Central America intellectuals are playing an important part in the framing process as they seek to link related ideologies, but the resulting mixture must be relevant to the needs of the people if it is to coalesce into an authentic movement. Among evangelicals this relevance is most often felt in supportive communities, in shared emotional experiences, and in a theology offering hope for the future.

First, we shall identify three major categories of Protestants and their distinguishing emphases, i.e., the divisive aspects of Protestantism. Then as we discuss the resources of the movement, we shall outline the most important commonalities of Protestantism that link together believers in the region. In examining the way Protestantism is being framed in Latin America, we need to focus on how it is distinct from what it is challenging, i.e., Catholicism and secularism. We will also focus on how the framing of Protestantism unites the various forms into a movement.

SHARED UNDERSTANDINGS
AND SOURCES OF DIVISION

There are four common defining frames of evangelicalism that "justify, dignify and animate collective action."[2] (1) Belief in a direct and personal relationship with Jesus Christ, the Son of God, that does not need mediation. "Belonging" occurs through personal acceptance of being "born again," which is symbolized in baptism, not through mediation by the Pope, saints, the pastor, or any other entity. (2) Belief in the Bible as the inerrant Word of God, as a strict guide to personal behavior, and as a book that should be widely translated and disseminated to all. (3) Emphasis on experiential religious encounters such as "speaking in tongues" received from the Holy Spirit (glossolalia) or faith healing. (4) Emphasis on an apocalyptic event related to the Second Coming of Christ. These shared meanings are widespread in Central America, even within denominations like the Presbyterians, most of whom practice a very different Reformed theology in the United States. We will examine certain divisions within the evangelical movement before we return to religious commonalities and the power of movement.

Belief in the Bible as the inerrant Word of God is the most potentially divisive issue in evangelical theological thought. Disagreement, of course, regularly occurs over biblical interpretation. Some Pentecostals, for instance, require the experience of speaking in tongues for full membership, whereas other more "moderate" Pentecostals value the experience without requiring it. Another dispute concerns the theology of the "Trinity," the traditional Christian belief in the Father, Son, and Holy Spirit, which most evangelicals accept. Some members such as the Pentecostal Church of God, however, are Unitarians and insist that Christians should reject the Trinity idea because it is not mentioned explicitly in the Bible.

Another complex debate, this one with more social and political implications, involves the proper role of evangelicals in approaching the problems of this world. Key texts for withdrawal from worldly concerns are Romans 13:1-6 ("Let every person be subject to the governing authorities, for there is no authority except from God, and those that exist have been instituted by God.") Matthew 22:15-22 ("Render therefore to Caesar the things that are Caesar's, and to God the things that are God's") and 1 John 2:15-17 ("Do not love the world . . ."; "The world passes away, and the lust of it; but he who does the will of God abides forever"). These scriptures are persuasive and authoritative frames that have justified an apolitical stance by many evangelicals within their troubled societies. Certainly some biblical passages could be interpreted as encouraging evangelicals to focus on the salvation of themselves and their loved ones and to pursue the "Kingdom of God, which is in Heaven." In many ways pursuing the heavenly Kingdom of God is easier and safer than addressing the intractable political and economic forces that also affect their daily lives.

In terms of social movement framing these biblical scriptures are both diagnostic and prescriptive. As sociologist Rhys H. Williams explains:

> Given that movements are collectivities in pursuit of change, their framing is often done in terms of a social, religious, or political "problem" that requires action. Movements rhetorically construct social problems through frames that define what the problem *is* ("diagnostic frames"), what should be *done* about it ("prescriptive frames"), who has the *responsibility* for doing it, and why action is *imperative* ("motivational frames").[3]

The diagnostic frame for many evangelicals, i.e.,"the problem," is personal ignorance or rejection of Christ and submission instead to worldly temptations. The prescription is therefore to accept Christ and to submit to his will for one's life. This is a personal, not a governmental, responsibility. This personalistic emphasis is what many scholarly critics point to as the quiescent aspect of evangelicalism that leads people to be passive and to accept the status quo when they "should" be politically active. But this criticism ignores the fact that the diagnosis and the prescription also have broad social ramifications for believers. *Society's* problems are diagnosed as being caused by sin, i.e., the widespread rejection of Christ. Thus *if everyone* accepted Christ's love and guidance, society would be improved, and (in the belief of many evangelicals) this would hasten the return of Christ to this world. The imperative, then, ("motivational frame") is for Protestants to spread the gospel, to hope for the Second Coming, and to support each other in daily struggles.

At a more subtle and gradual level of daily religious practice, Protestantism has a potential link to society and politics that has been recognized since the Reformation. The belief in an unmediated contact with God and the widespread availability of the Bible were challenges to the authority of the Roman Catholic Church. Thus the Protestant Reformation framing of a "priesthood of all believers" who could discern the will of God through engagement with Scripture, guided by the Holy Spirit, provided the rationale for empowerment of both individuals and communities of faith—and still does. Its social power is manifest when individuals engage in interactive, interdependent religious communities. Importantly, emphasis on a personal, unmediated relationship with Christ is a unifying element of evangelical beliefs, a point of deep and widespread agreement.

It does not require much of an analytical stretch to ascertain the egalitarian and democratizing aspects of elevating lay church members to a "priesthood." The most obvious examples of such democratization in a Central American context are the leadership opportunities in Pentecostal churches that are available to the poorest illiterate members who have eloquence and "gifts from the Spirit." Unlike the hierarchical demands of Catholicism or the seminary requirements of some mainline Protestants, most evangelical congregations only require their pastor to have the gift of the Spirit. This is a highly flexible system, appropriate for a society in which a majority of the people are poor and illiterate. Even women—who are often excluded from male-dominated church institutions—can gain authority in these churches through their biblical expertise or spiritual gifts. For instance, the most respected member I met at the Church of the New Jerusalem in a small town in Guatemala was not the pastor, but a woman who regularly practiced faith healing and speaking in tongues.

As sociologist David Martin notes, "[T]he crucial characteristic of evangelical Christianity in the vast urban [and rural] agglomerations of Latin America is self-government. People are able to devise their own social world for themselves."[4] It has long been argued that Protestantism during the Reformation planted the seeds for participatory democracy as a form of government. At this point we are not talking about explicit political organizations or attitudes (chapter 5). Rather, we are noting the gradual process of grassroots empowerment that can begin with collective action frames that are not only nonhierarchical, but elevate the poorest individuals to persons in direct contact with God. It is difficult to imagine a more empowering belief system.

The apocalyptic belief in hastening the Second Coming of Christ is a heartfelt motivational frame for millions of evangelicals. It is further delineated in a school of theology called Dispensationalism, which has been mostly widely disseminated by the Dallas Theological Seminary (through the Scofield reference Bible) and the Central American Mission. Because CAM was one of the first and most successful faith missions, as we saw in the preceding chapter, Dispensationalism is particularly widespread in the region. The belief is that history is divided into seven time periods or dispensations during which humans must pass a specific test of obedience to God. The dispensations are as follows:

Innocence (Eden; Genesis 1:28)
Conscience (Fall to Noah; Genesis 3:23)
Human Government (Noah to Abraham; Genesis 8:21)
Promise (Abraham to Moses; Genesis 12:1)
Law (Moses to Christ; Exodus 19:8)
Grace (Church Age, between Christ's two comings; John 1:17)
Kingdom (millennium, after Christ's return; Ephesians 1:10)[5]

The belief is that currently Christians are in the period of Grace, and their task is to evangelize every person on the planet, to give everyone an opportunity to accept Christianity before Christ's Second Coming. This return event is imminent and will bring in a thousand years of perfect peace and justice for Christians, known as the Millennium. Thus, Dispensationalism is "premillennial," teaching that Christ will come again *before* the thousand-year reign of peace, and that Christians will be rescued to heaven in what is called the Rapture. These believers quote Matthew 24:14 ("And this gospel of the kingdom will be preached throughout the whole world, as a testimony to all nations; and then the end will come"). They also put special emphasis on the Bible's apocalyptic literature such as chapters of Daniel, Ezekiel, Paul's epistles (especially Thessalonians), and the book of Revelation. These beliefs help to explain why premillennial evangelicals proselytize so eagerly. They believe that their task is to convert as many individuals as possible to true Christianity and then to wait for Christ's return.[6]

Another position, which allows for more deliberate social and political activism, has been gaining credence among evangelicals, especially those of the middle and upper classes in Central America. This is the "postmillennialist" view that Christ will return *after* a thousand-year reign by Christians. The belief is that this reign may have begun already. Signs of it may be steady progress for Christians in politics, in the economy, and in society as a whole. In this scenario the task for Christians is to ensure and hasten the Second Coming by working for material and political goals as well as spiritual ones. Some of these believers equate progress with improvements in commerce; thus they elevate business success to a messianic purpose that has a powerful motivational impact. Whereas Max Weber identified Calvinist Protestantism as a source of the capitalist motive, this postmillennial, emotional theology may have a more significant effect on the behavior of its followers than Calvinism.[7]

In addition to apocalyptic passages, other powerful scriptures specifically direct Christian involvement in social concerns and counteract the detachment of some evangelicals. For instance, Jesus's directive in Matthew 25:31-46 ("as you did it to one of the least of these my brethren, you did it to me") and the poetry of Luke 4:18-19:

> The Spirit of the Lord is upon me,
> because he has anointed me to preach
>   good news to the poor.
> He has sent me to proclaim release of
>   the captives
> and recovering of sight to the blind,
> to set at liberty those who are oppressed,
> to proclaim the acceptable year of the Lord.

The Luke passage is often cited as a key inspirational passage for liberation theology, but it is important to remember that many Protestants as well as Catholics have been proponents of this particular theology. The Bible, after all, is nondenominational. Let us try to make some sense of the incredible Protestant diversity before continuing the discussion of framing.

1) The *Traditionalists* include the historic Protestant churches that first met at the Congress of Panama in 1916. They now comprise the smallest of the three major groups. Their influence, however, belies their numbers because their leaders are more likely to disseminate published works on society and politics as well as sermons and theology. These evangelicals are American Baptists, Presbyterians, Methodists, Episcopalians, Lutherans and a few other smaller denominations. They do not engage in the emotional worship style of testimony and glossolalia (speaking in tongues from the Holy Spirit). The Traditionalists also refer to themselves as the "progressive" branch of Protestantism in Central America and are more likely to be ecumenical than other Protestants in terms of their association with many Catholics. As progressives, they are also more likely than most Pentecostals to protest human rights violations in a direct way. We have already noted the Presbyterian human rights workers who were killed for their activism in Guatemala by a death squad linked to the military in 1994 and 1995.[8] These particular denominational leaders often network with national, regional, and international human rights organizations.

2) The *Pentecostals* are concentrated in the poorest urban areas and in rural sectors. They are Fundamentalists, i.e., they believe in Biblical inerrancy and in the importance of personal "born-again" experiences for religious conversion. They practice highly-charged worship services with much singing, faith healing, and glossolalia. As noted, a few of the Pentecostals require a

speaking in tongues experience for full membership in their church. A large majority of Central American Protestants are Pentecostals; for example, they make up around 80 percent of Nicaraguan Protestants.[9] They are by far the fastest growing group of evangelicals and include many denominations and faith missions, the largest being the Assembly of God.

3) The *neo-Pentecostals* are found primarily in urban areas and have grown in number among working-class, middle-class, and upper-class professionals. Many of their leaders are trained in the U.S. The major difference between them and the Pentecostals is their attitude toward material well-being. To generalize, the poorest Pentecostals adapt to their situation by denying the importance of the material world whereas the neo-Pentecostals believe that God will reward good Christians with material wealth. They are also the group most likely to accept postmillenial beliefs that the world will improve before Christ's return and that they should be involved in the economy and national politics to hasten that event. The neo-Pentecostals are the most upwardly mobile of the three groups.[10] But it should also be noted that the majority of these neo-Pentecostals were *already* in the middle and upper classes when they converted. They include such churches as Frontera Cristiani, Shaddhai, Maranatha, the Full Gospel Businessmen's Fellowship, and the Elim Church (which includes more working-class members). One careful observer of these categories speculates that many members of the neo-Pentecostal groups were wealthier Catholics who converted because they felt betrayed by the attacks of liberation theology on the economic system.[11] For obvious class reasons they have little contact with the majority of Pentecostals, who are the urban and rural poor.

UNIFYING FRAMES OF PROTESTANTISM

On the surface the evangelical presence in Latin America is extremely fragmented, but I argue that the fragmentation is an overlay of the unifying themes we have examined and that its divisive impact has been exaggerated. The most significant division is the one between the neo-Pentecostal churches and the others because that fissure occurs along class lines; yet even these groups find points of agreement with other Protestants. As noted previously,

the surface fragmentation has favored the growth of Protestantism because the movement spreads through the process of decentralization as people "shop" in the new religious marketplace for
a church that is meaningful to them or as they establish a brand
new one. Thus a pragmatic reason for the wildfire-like spread of
evangelicalism is the ease of forming new churches. As sociologist David Martin notes, it is the *combination* of the North American pattern of religion with Latin cultures in ways that are
"endlessly inventive" that gives the evangelical movement its ex-
pansive power.[12] There are at least one hundred different Protestant denominations or faith missions in each country (at least three
hundred in Guatemala). They are primarily Pentecostal, but the
specific variations that divide them are less significant than the
similarities that unify them into a movement.

Field observation gives evidence of this close interaction among
the variety of Protestants—for instance, in the binding symbolism
of referring to all fellow evangelicals as "brothers" and "sisters."
We have outlined the theology of Dispensationalism that is loose-
ly adhered to by many evangelicals; however, the details of these
teachings, i.e., the particular dispensations, seem unimportant. As
one minister in El Salvador explained his beliefs,

> I don't care if the Lord is coming or if He will scratch everything
> with one simple act of His will, or if it will be a process. I don't
> care. What I need to care about is being closer to Him. And if I'm
> closer to Him everything will be for the good. So I'm not worried
> about that. Yes, we have a statement about the Rapture, but we work
> with a lot of churches, so we don't really teach that.[13]

This lack of concern about precise theology was a typical feature
of interviews with religious leaders and church members, and
matches the lack of concern with written doctrines and creeds.

In an anthropological study of Mayan widows in Guatemala
Linda Green notes that the women move back and forth between
various evangelical churches in their community. In a typical case
Antonia, a widow with eight sons, meets with a Bible study group
that discusses social injustices, but she is also the member of the
Church of God, which meets nightly for highly spiritual *cultos*
(worship services). Green concludes that the churches meet wom-
en's needs only partially, so they "cross religious boundaries"

easily to meet other needs.[14] However, in terms of a social movement, Green's observation is important for highlighting the underlying unity of Protestantism that is not as fragmented as the panoply of church names might indicate. A church scholar in Nicaragua pointed out that not only do members shift affiliations, "many pastors have jumped from one denomination to another, from one role to another. It's a free-wheeling situation."[15]

The pattern of open-mindedness is frequently found within individual churches as well. For instance, one former Methodist missionary to Central America who strongly supports the goals of liberation theology explained that he had come to accept the "holiness approach to the expression of faith because if you don't connect emotionally with the people, you retreat completely into your religion." He stated that his wish as a pastor in Central America was to "wean the people away from Revelation and toward Matthew, Mark, Luke, and John," i.e., the more socially activist portions of the Bible.[16] This particular missionary had spent enough time in Central America to understand the appeal of Pentecostalism, even though he disagreed with much of its theology. He was not concerned with upholding traditional Methodist doctrine. Such disparities between the theological leanings of church members and denominational leaders are commonplace.

The softening of religious doctrines and creeds is by no means unique to Protestants in Central America. Religious sociologist Robert Wuthnow has analyzed the impact of declining denominationalism within the United States and notes the following indicators: "increased interfaith and interdenominational switching, heightened tolerance across faiths and denominational boundaries, ecumenical cooperation, and a de-emphasis in many denominations on distinctive teachings and specific membership requirements."[17] All of these indicators are evident in the Protestant missionary field and among evangelicals in Central America as well.[18] Wuthnow's point about this development in the United States is that "declining denominationalism has made it easier for mobilization to occur across group boundaries."[19] A similar observation can be made about the social movement aspect of Protestantism in Central America. The boundaries in this supposedly fragmented movement are extremely porous, and informal alliances are as easily formed as more formal ones, as we shall see in chapter 5.

HOW EVANGELICAL FRAMING OCCURS
AND ITS IMPACT AT THE MICROLEVEL

It has been our primary purpose to examine the implications of Protestant success in Central America, not to focus on *why* Protestantism has been so successful. But as we move into a discussion of how evangelical framing occurs, we gain insight into some of the reasons for the popularity of the movement. With other observers we note that the growth rates that have made the last thirty years more significant than previous evangelical surges in the region began precisely when Protestantism became more Pentecostal, i.e., more experiential and emotional in style.[20] Quentin J. Schultze emphasizes the oral tradition of Pentecostalism, as opposed to literacy, as the key to its particular success:

> It appears that Latin American Pentecostalism is highly oral, and that its orality has meshed extremely effectively with the indigenous orality of the region as well a with the particular needs of the urban poor. This is not to say that orality *caused* the explosion of Pentecostalism in Latin America. Rather, I wish to argue that the largely oral character of culture among Latin America's poor is a necesary but not sufficient prerequisite to the growth of traditional Pentecostalism.[21]

He points out that the orality is reinforced by religious broadcasts on radio and television that are extremely popular throughout Central America. (It is important to note, however, that religious broadcasting is rarely a source of conversion. Rather, it is primarily a source of entertainment and inspiration for those who are already Pentecostals.)[22] Furthermore, the oral nature of Pentecostalism is another factor contributing to declining denominationalism, discussed previously. Denominations are defined and organized in writing, but Pentecostal church members do not pledge themselves to distinctive written doctrines. They simply give oral testimonies of their beliefs before the community. As Schultze writes, "Perhaps the most obvious and significant characteristic of an oral culture is the high level of shared life. While print tends to enhance individualization, specialization, and rationalization, orality necessarily promotes localized common cultures."[23]

The impact of music is a neglected factor in analyses of Pentecostalism. When the oral framing of evangelical beliefs and priorities are set to music, they are even more powerful, particularly for attracting and holding younger members. One Protestant liberation theologian, dismayed by the anti-intellectualism of the Pentecostals, said the music was "like a drug."[24] But another observer, a minister with the Christian Missionary Alliance, noted that "the music fits the hearts of the people. Music is 80 to 85 percent of the message."[25] The music is rhythmic and the words are repetitive, and easy to sing. They reflect a simple theology, as illustrated in these popular hymn titles: "Nuevas Alegres!" ("Joyful News!"); "Señor, quien entrara?" ("Señor, who will enter?" "el Señor" is a reference to Jesus Christ often heard in Latin America); and "Bendito es el Señor, la Roca de mi salvación" ("Blessed is the Señor, the Rock of my salvation").[26] Pentecostal services are often standing room only, and characterized by all the anticipation and excitement of rock concerts with spirituality. In nations where majorities of the population face oppressive poverty and millions have been displaced to alien urban settings, such events are uplifting respites.

Tomás, a young member of the Church of the New Jerusalem, described for me the weekly services held in his Guatemalan town:

> We meet on Wednesdays, Saturdays, and Sundays. We have over three hundred members and everyone is active! On Wednesdays, it is only for the youth, with much music and singing. I myself play guitar and drums, and I am learning the trumpet. On Sundays it is for everyone. We do not eat breakfast, and no lunch, and we meet from eight in the morning until seven at night. How long is that? Yes, eleven hours. There is no music on Sundays, only prayer and healing and the Spirit speaking through people. One woman has much faith and she always speaks. Yes, I can understand her inside my head and my heart. Afterwards we all have supper together.[27]

I found that highly participatory meetings two or three times a week are the rule for Pentecostals, not the exception. One of the few sources of empirical data on the topic support this impression: two national surveys in El Salvador found that evangelicals attend worship services twice as frequently as active Catholics: 9.27 times per month versus 4.66 times per month. One-third of the evangelicals surveyed attend three times a week, and 12 percent worship at church daily.[28]

The impact of these services for socializing and community-building is significant, but this religious approach also touches the people's family lives because it is combined with belief in the Bible as a strict guidebook for behavior. As an illustration, I recall a devoutly evangelical family in Costa Rica. Typically, Flora Isabel and her husband José were from Catholic families. Flora's grandmother was still a practicing Catholic, even though most of her family had converted to the new religion. Flora had visited the Iglesia de Cristo in a suburb of San José with a female friend and had been profoundly touched by the warmth of the people and the enthusiasm of the services in contrast to the sparsely attended Catholic services. She joined the church after intense prayers and baptism by immersion. Flora and her husband had two small sons at that time and were having financial difficulties because José was only employed sporadically and frequently spent his income in nightclubs. Flora worked as a housekeeper. She prayed constantly for José's conversion to Protestantism and begged him to accompany her to church. Eventually he did so, and he was soon converted. The church loaned the family money to buy a car and José got a license and a steady position as a government chauffeur, which enabled the family to buy a home. Now the whole family usually attends church two or three times each week, including a monthly all-night vigil of prayer that is held for church members who are suffering. Flora and her youngest son prepared food eagerly for this vigil and spent ten hours with other church members deeply engaged in an experience they described as "very beautiful, very spiritual." Thus the church remains the center of life for this family—spiritually, socially, and psychologically. They credit Christ and the church with their family's current emotional and financial stability, including home ownership. Much of their enthusiasm and faith is motivated by gratitude.

Although the experience of Flora and José occurred in a working-class suburb of San José, Costa Rica, the pattern is very similar in rural areas of Guatemala and presumably elsewhere. Several studies by sociologists confirm that it is the usual pattern for women to convert first to Protestantism.[29] The women desire to bring stability to the family, to counter the destructive aspects of *machismo*, and to find support in times of political violence and poverty, all highly rational, pragmatic motivations. The person who converts to Protestantism typically embarks on a course of self-improvement and strict personal morality, often in a direct challenge to secularism.

For instance, an indigenous family of two adults, grandmother, and four children in Pastores, Guatemala, also experienced dramatic transformation after Ana introduced her husband to the evangelical church. When asked why he converted, he indicated that his wife had brought him there because of his drinking problem. He now preaches at his own *Asambleas de Dios* church in the agricultural village of Pastores, and he acknowledges that he is very happy now, that life is better. Constructed with a simple sheet-metal roof and situated precariously on the hillside, the church contains a few benches and is furnished with a rough pulpit and an electronic megaphone through which the preacher broadcasts his sermon. This innovation allows the people to continue their daily chores while he preaches—and also prevents easy escape from his inspired message!

The churches provide supportive communities that encourage personal reform, a point that is often overlooked when scholars emphasize the individualism often associated with Protestantism. One early study by Bryan R. Roberts found that low-income Protestants in Guatemala City taught each other household budgeting and also provided mutual assistance to brothers and sisters in need. "Should a Protestant in one of the neighborhoods need help to improve or repair his house, install drainage, or obtain a loan, other members of his congregation join together to give help. If a Protestant is out of a job or wants to change his work, other members of his congregation help him find work."[30] I discovered a similar attitude when visiting the slums and dumps of Guatemala City with the Protestant pastor who directed a project for the *Áreas Marginales* (marginal areas). We visited small bakeries and neighborhood stores that had received seed money from the churches, as well as an oasis of several concrete block homes in the slums that members had joined together to build.

This supportive characteristic of many of the urban Protestant churches has also been identified in remote areas of the countryside. Green's study of Mayan women in a rural area of Guatemala where many of the men had been killed in political violence found similar church community:

> The nightly services allow women a safe haven to participate in com-
> munal activities. . . . they provide pleasurable diversion with the clap-
> ping, shouting, and praying. Church members also help each other,
> work together to build houses, plant and harvest corn. *Cultos* [ser-
> vices] provide a place and space within which to rebuild a sense of
> trust and community. . . . The women talk about their suffering and
> sorrows, and they look for ways in which they can work together to
> change their situation.[31]

Evangelical churches are the central institutions of this Mayan
village and provide the women with "a mechanism to recapture
control over their lives."[32]

The strict lifestyle stressed by the Protestant churches dove-
tails with the emphasis on saving. Numerous anthropological studies of Latin American locations have documented the difference
that Protestant conversion makes in the struggle against extreme
poverty, as the converts are able to save money when they ab-
stain from alcohol and from the traditional festivals. (In fact, the
consistency of the findings raises the question again of why political science has so long neglected analysis of the fact that religion *matters* as a distinctive force for social mobility.)[33] Thus a
less expensive lifestyle, a strict belief system, and a supportive
community allow many Protestant families to reallocate their meager resources. Interestingly, I spoke with employers in Guatemala
who indicated that the good reputation of the evangelicals was
also helping them economically. One prominent businessman was
unrestrained in voicing his opinion:

> I have seventy employees, and I can tell you the evangelicals are more
> productive, more trustworthy, the better employees. The first thing
> the evangelicals do is have an impact on alcoholism, and that's the
> biggest problem in this country! You can go to any hospital and that's
> why the majority of the people are there. Around these evangelicals,
> prosperity begins to bloom.[34]

Anthropologist Sheldon Annis has conducted the most detailed
study of religion and microlevel change in Guatemala in his book,
God and Production in a Guatemalan Town.[35] Annis combines
participant observation with survey research uncovering the family economies of residents of San Antonio Aguas Calientes, Guatemala. Although his original research was about migratory labor
and land distribution, Annis learned that the factor most predic-

tive of which families would be upwardly mobile was Protestantism. This was not because the evangelicals worked harder than
Catholics, but because they were highly motivated to *save*—even
pennies a day—to improve their lives in a material way that would
parallel their spiritual rebirth. The most common phrase heard
among the many evangelicals in the town was "*del suelo al cielo*," or "from the dirt floor to the sky; from rags to riches." Annis recounts several *del suelo al cielo* stories, as evangelicals were
able to save money because they gave up alcohol, luxuries, and
costly traditional festivals. He found that overall, average Catholic wealth was only 81 percent of the average Protestant wealth,
and that Protestants were more than twice as likely as Catholics
to own a vehicle. Furthermore, Protestants showed more future
orientation than Catholics because the Protestant children were
more likely to go to school and Protestants were more likely to
work in upwardly mobile occupations leading to small business
ownership (e.g., tailoring, tourism, transportation, etc.). The Catholic families in the town tended to work in subsistence farming,
primarily planting corn. Protestants who remained in agriculture,
however, used more advanced farming techniques, planted high-
yielding commodities and fared better than Catholics in almost
every measure of agricultural productivity.[36] He found similar
patterns in comparing textile entrepreneurship between Catholic
and Protestant women—the evangelical women were more successful at making money from the sale of their weavings.[37]

Annis's research is not normative—he documents and analyzes
the economic structure of the town as a scholar. If anything, he
regrets the cultural changes that Protestantism is reinforcing. He
writes poignantly about how Protestant women in the Mayan towns
are less likely to wear the exquisitely woven blouses (*huipils*) and
about how the Protestants weave more for sale to tourists than
for tradition. However, two points must be made. First, Protestantism is not the cause of the macrolevel forces that are bearing
down on the people of these towns—the decades-long civil war,
the agro-export economy, and the influx of tourism that are inev-
itably disrupting the cultural stability of traditional Catholicism
and subsistence farming. Second, a certain condescension is implicit in the nostalgia scholars may feel regarding changes occurring in a unique culture. No matter how deeply we as observers

may regret the cultural struggle, the simple fact is that many indigenous people are choosing to be evangelicals for a reason, and
it is hoped that social scientists will respect these choices. One
apparent appeal of Protestantism at the microlevel is its practical
theology that gives the people a tool for adapting and even prevailing in the midst of massive changes going on around them.

This interpretation makes even more sense when one considers
the weaknesses of the present-day Catholic Church in Central
America, which we will address in chapter 4. Converts pragmat-
ically choose to leave the Catholic Church because it no longer
meets their needs. The Roman Catholic Church has longevity in
Central America, but it also has become weak, inflexible, and
understaffed. Over two-thirds of the clergy of the Guatemalan
Catholic Church are foreigners. The bishop of the Diocese of
Sololá wearily stated that he had only fifty-two priests for a population of nine hundred thousand, and ten of the priests were
American missionaries. He acknowledged that the Catholic Church
neglected its pastoral duties because of the shortage of clergy and
also because of complacency.[38] Similarly, in Nicaragua, the head
of a prominent Protestant organization noted that there were fewer than five hundred priests in Nicaragua and most of them were
foreign, whereas his organization alone had twenty-two hundred
pastors and worked in over three hundred villages where there were
no priests.[39] This neglect is one reason that only approximately
15 percent of avowed Catholics are active participants.[40] Thus
many of the comparisons between Protestants and Catholics in this
section are in reality between religious practitioners and nonprac-
titioners.

A debate often arises in discussions of Latin American Protestantism between the view that conversion *leads* to social mobility
and the view that a self-selecting variable is at work here: people
who convert are particularly open to change and innovation in
general, and this attitude itself helps them raise their standard of
living in changing times. Some immeasurable degree of self-selec-
tion is probably operating, but, based on primary and secondary
research, the present analysis opts strongly for the view that conversion itself encourages social mobility. This view is persuasive
because of the coalescence of several factors inherent in these
churches that help to alleviate poverty. For instance, the primary

approach is not to provide direct aid, but to encourage change in individual behavior in the context of a spiritual community. Churches expect members to adopt ascetic, disciplined lifestyles, including abstaining from sexual promiscuity and alcohol. But members are not alone in the quest for a changed material and spiritual life. They participate in church fellowship, often nightly services with spirited singing and socializing that replace the now unacceptable practices. It is in the community setting that members hear repeatedly the diagnostic, prescriptive, and imperative framing of the ideology: that with faith and disciplined lives they can help bring God's plan into fruition. Furthermore, they have role models all around them of people who have worked hard and succeeded. It is a crucial point that these role models are their peers, with similar backgrounds of oppression and hardship. It should not be surprising that the members of these churches know the most effective ways to comfort, discipline, assist, and motivate their members. Thus the churches teach attitudinal and behavioral change in the setting of a close-knit group of "brothers" and "sisters" going through the same process—a powerful combination.

In an essay reviewing ten books that implicitly address the process of symbolic framing and the societal impact of religion, Daniel Levine summarizes their similar conclusion:

> [Religion has] a tremendous *consolidating* power. I refer to the peculiar ability of religious metaphors, places, and rituals to sum up and intensify experience. They do this by joining everyday events to a sense of supernatural intervention and by reinforcing religious ideas with material resources and a net of repeated human interactions. This is what religious organizations and rituals *do*, and this is why they are so powerful at unifying behavior across social levels and in different arenas and walks of life.[41]

The "tremendous *consolidating* power" of religion and a "net of repeated human interactions" are aspects of building a movement. All of the authors Levine reviews took the microlevel approach in their research and analysis, agreeing that examining politics and religion and social programs from the macrolevel had missed the more subtle and deep-seated changes that occurred "from below." They demonstrate how "the search for meaning and control goes on in the spaces available in everyday life," and they concur that religion "can provide a seedbed for new kinds of leadership and solidarities."[42]

A NEW STAGE FOR THE
PROTESTANT MOVEMENT

Scholars have produced analyses of Protestant growth in Latin America, but field observations and some data also indicate a slowing of the evangelical movement. The most frequently cited study is by Protestant missionary, John Kessler. Kessler analyzes the results of two religious surveys conducted in Costa Rica by independent researchers. The first 1989 survey, indicated that 8.1 percent of the adult population of Costa Rica had left a Protestant church, most returning to Catholicism, but 31 percent of those dropping out of religious exercise altogether. In a repeat survey in 1991 the percentage of those responding that they had left Protestantism rose to 12.1 percent.[43]

Interviews with some Protestant leaders support this evidence of declining levels of commitment. The director of the Campus Crusade for Christ in San Salvador, for instance, made the following analysis about the urban church:

> I think that evangelical churches have a problem—that all social groups find. This is when the quantity goes up, the quality goes down. . . . We are only gaining people who are very comfortable—people who do not have a higher aspiration. They attend evangelical church as they attended Catholic Church—just for the sake of attending but without a commitment. . . . Thirty years ago, to say you were a evangelical was to be a martyr—you could die. But now it isn't that way. . . . So the quality of the members of the evangelical church has diminished because anyone can call himself evangelical.[44]

Along the same lines Roy Peterson of Wycliffe Bible Translators in Guatemala observed that "evangelicalism has grown so fast, people aren't integrating it into their lives the way they used to. It's an infant religion; it's like they're running around in diapers."[45] David Stoll describes his encounter with upwardly mobile members of a particular Assembly of God church in Guatemala. Few people were present in the new church building because, as the members explained, the young people preferred rock music and television to worship.[46]

How do we explain the contradictory evidence of Protestant health and continued growth versus early signs of stagnation and decline in Central America? I would speculate that the most influential variable behind the decline of some evangelical churches and the continued vitality of others is the social class of the churches. That is, the evangelical churches that are the most upwardly mobile and closest to the secular attractions of the middle and upper classes are most likely to be experiencing signs of stagnation, particularly among the young. Testing this hypothesis would require detailed surveys comparing churches of various economic strata and controlling for many factors such as pastoral training, age of the church, external environment, etc. In the absence of extensive surveys this view is put forth based on observation of churches of different social strata in Central America—the poorest churches seem to have the largest numbers of committed members. It also follows from this hypothesis that Costa Rica, which enjoys the highest per capita income in Central America, would be the nation most likely to have a high evangelical "drop-out" rate as less committed members drift to secular activities when their initial interest fades. In contrast, in extremely poor villages and urban neighborhoods one finds that the participatory services are not only spiritual experiences but are places for entertainment and socializing as well.

Thus some evangelical churches face the challenge of preserving the gains they have so recently made in Central America. The Protestant movement is decidedly entering the new phase of consolidation described in social movement literature. As social movements evolve, they must develop their own resources and draw on existing resources in the broader society in order to maintain and strengthen themselves. This is the dynamic of becoming bureaucratized and professionalized for the sake of the survival of the movement.[47] In chapter 5 we will examine how some movement leaders are attempting to organize the movement to enter the political realm. There is considerable risk in this kind of institutionalization because it can dilute the strength and spontaneity of the movement. But sociologist Rhys H. Williams, for one, is impressed with the survivability of all fundamentalist movements, including evangelicalism in Central America:

> Fundamentalist [social movement organizations] must develop organizational mechanisms to negotiate the tension between stasis and change, avoiding the Scylla of stagnation and the Charybdis of accommodation. . . . [t]he fact that so many fundamentalist movement organizations have successfully managed organizational flexibility without sacrificing ideological distinctiveness is testimony to the creative capacity of human innovation.[48]

One can hypothesize that once the evangelical church leaders who are struggling with membership accept the continuing pull of secular/consumer temptations, they will become more adept at competing with them, as have many churches in the U.S. For instance, we have already noted the power and popularity of praise music in most services. The Campus Crusade for Christ director in San Salvador, concerned about apathetic members, was actively promoting an Athletes in Action program with Christian soccer and wrestling teams. He was also setting up family counseling support groups in his church, an example of explicit efforts to meet the desires of the community. Related to these types of adjustments is the growing number of evangelical seminaries within Central America, and the development of a written evangelical theology which was referenced at the beginning of the chapter. For instance, the Secretary General of the respected *Centro InterEclesial de Estudios Teológicos y Sociales (CIEETS)* in Managua, Nicaragua explains the work of his institution.

> We teach the history of the church and we emphasize evangelicalism, but are also ecumenical. Protestant church leaders in Nicaragua, even Pentecostals, are eager to train and to learn. We have 600 students and would have 1,000 if we had the capacity, so we compensate with workshops. Pentecostals have more confidence now and are coming for training.[49]

Sidney Tarrow concurs with Williams that, even as they become institutionalized, religious movements have particular advantages as a sustaining base for social movements:

> [L]eaders can only create a social movement when they tap more deep-rooted feelings of solidarity or identity. This is almost certainly why nationalism and ethnicity—based on real or "imagined" ties— *or religion—based on common devotion—have been more reliable bases of movement organization in the past than social class.*[50] (emphasis added)

Thus we return to the point that Protestantism in Central America shows a superficial fragmentation that often conceals its underlying unity. Although middle-class Pentecostal churches are especially challenged by secularism and are losing marginal members, a sense of common devotion instills a solidarity among committed evangelicals that is deeper than class ties or class distinctions. We should be careful not to make the mistake of underestimating the endurance of religion in the face of modernization, as many scholars did when they predicted the demise of religiosity in the United States. The common devotion experienced by evangelicals in Central America is powerful—sustained by familiar social networks and framed in song and Scripture.

NOTES

1. David Snow, Burke E. Rochford Jr., Steven K. Worden, and Robert D. Benford, "Frame Alignment Processes, Micromobilization, and Movement Participation," *American Sociological Review* 51 (1986): 464.

2. Sidney Tarrow, *Power in Movement: Social Movements, Collective Action and Politics* (New York: Cambridge University Press, 1994), 22.

3. Rhys H. Williams, "Movement Dynamics and Social Change: Transforming Fundamentalist Ideology and Organizations," in *Accounting for Fundamentalisms: The Dynamic Character of Movements*, ed. Martin E. Marty and R. Scott Appleby (Illinois: University of Chicago Press, 1994), 791.

4. David Martin, *Tongues of Fire: The Explosion of Protestantism in Latin America* (London: Basil Blackwell, 1990), 285.

5. Vern S. Poythress, *Understanding Dispensationalists* (Grand Rapids, Mich.: Zondervan, 1987), 21. Also see Timothy P. Weber, "Dispensationalism," in *A New Handbook of Christian Theology*, ed. Donald W. Musser and J. L. Price (Nashville: Abingdon, 1992), 125–127. Weber notes the process of revisionism in which some dispensational theologians are questioning the significance of Israel and the church, the need to interpret the Bible literally, and the appropriateness of stressing dispensations in history at all. "In short," he writes, "if the current revisionism continues, dispensationalists will find it difficult to distinguish themselves from other kinds of conservative and evangelical theologians." This softening of teaching among theologians coincides with the lack of concern about historical periods and bibli-

cal inerrancy that I have encountered in Central American churches. On the other hand, imprecise references to the "Second Coming" and the "Kingdom" are pervasive.

6. Dennis A. Smith, "The Gospel according to the United States: Evangelical Broadcasting in Central America," in *American Evangelicals and the Mass Media,* ed. Quentin Schultze (Grand Rapids, Mich.: Academie Books, Zondervan, 1990), 289–306.

7. Smith, "The Gospel," 294; Madonna-Claire Kolbenschlag, "The Protestant Ethic and Evangelical Capitalism: The Weberian Thesis Revisited," *Southern Quarterly,* July 1976, 14, 287–306.

8. Alexa Smith, "Presbyterians Sought as International Witnesses to Guatemalan Violence," *The News of the Presbyterian Church U.S.A.,* September 1995, 1.

9. Benjamín Cortés, Professor and Secretary General, Centro InterEclesial de Estudios Teológicos y Sociales (CIEETS), interview with author, Managua, Nicaragua, 12 November 1993.

10. Smith, "Gospel," 293–95. In an interview with Smith regarding neo-Pentecostals, he elaborated with disdain, "They see the church as a platform for increased consumerism and they preach a gospel of success, that you have a right to take God by the throat and force him to bless you!"

11. Dennis A. Smith, Latin American Evangelical Center for Pastoral Studies (CELEP), interview with author, Guatemala City, 16 January 1995.

12. Martin, *Tongues of Fire,* 295.

13. Enrique Nuncio, Director of Campus Crusade for Christ, interview with author, San Salvador, El Salvador, 19 January 1995.

14. Linda Green, "Shifting Affiliations: Mayan Widows and *Evangélicos* in Guatemala," in Garrard-Burnett and Stoll, *Rethinking Protestantism,* 172–75.

15. Jorge Bardeguez, Antonio Valdivieso Ecumenical Center (CAV), interview with author, Managua, Nicaragua, 9 November 1993.

16. Joseph Eldridge, United Methodist Church, interview with author, Washington, D.C., 8 June 1990.

17. Robert Wuthnow, "The Future of the Religious Right," in *No Longer Exiles: The Religious New Right in American Politics,* ed. Michael Cromartie (Washington, D.C.: Ethics and Public Policy Center, 1993), 33. Also see Wuthnow's analysis of declining denominationalism in the U.S. in *The Restructuring of American Religion: Society and Faith Since World War II* (Princeton: Princeton University Press, 1988).

18. John A. Siewert and John A. Kenyon, eds., *Mission Handbook: 1993–95* (Monrovia, Calif.: Mission Advanced Research Center/

WorldVision International, 1993), 6. The authors note that supporters now give more money to nondenominational agencies than to the institutional church.

19. Wuthnow, "Future," 33.

20. Martin, *Tongues of Fire,* 285. As we noted in chapter 1, Martin and David Stoll's *Is Latin America Turning Protestant?* (Los Angeles: University of California Press, 1990) survey the diverse literature examining the reasons for conversion—because of aggressive missionaries, local autonomy, active laity, egalitarianism, anomie, displacement, erosion of Catholicism, cultural affinity, mutual aid, etc.

21. Quentin J. Schultze, "Orality and Power in Latin American Pentecostalism," in *Coming of Age: Protestantism in Contemporary Latin America*, ed. Daniel R. Miller (Lanham, Md.: University Press of America, 1994), 83.

22. Smith, "Gospel," 302–3.

23. Schultze, "Orality," 81. In conjunction with the oral and musical framing of theology, the use of pictures is widespread among evangelicals. For example, members of the Four Square Pentecostal church frequently preach in village squares and on street corners using large colorful posters to illustrate their points. In Guatemala, I have witnessed largely Mayan audiences being enthralled by these dramatic pictures illustrating Old Testament stories or the apocalyptic book of Revelations. The framing of Pentecostalism using colorful symbols is somewhat similar to the framing of ancient Mayan religions.

24. Otto Minerva, Academic Vice President, Seminario Biblio Latinoamericano, interview with author, San Jose, Costa Rica, 26 July 1993.

25. Reverend Dale Whitman, Christian Missionary Alliance, interview with author, DeLand, Florida, 20 November 1995.

26. Hymn titles from "Hymns of the Christian Life."

27. Tomás, interview with author, San Antonio Agua Calientes, Guatemala, 14 July 1995.

28. Kenneth M. Coleman et al., "Protestantism in El Salvador: Conventional Wisdom versus the Survey Evidence," in *Rethinking Protestantism in Latin America*, ed. Virginia Garrard-Burnett and David Stoll (Philadelphia: Temple University Press, 1993), 119–20.

29. Elizabeth Brusco, "The Reformation of Machismo: Asceticism and Masculinity among Colombian Evangelicals," in Garrard-Burnett and Stoll, *Rethinking Protestantism*, 143–58; Green, "Shifting Affiliations"; John Burdick, "Rethinking the Study of Social Movements: The Case of Christian Base Communities in Urban Brazil," in *New Social Movements in Latin America: Identity, Strategy, and Democracy*, ed.

Sonio Alvarez and Arturo Escobar (Boulder, Colo.: Westview, 1992), 171–84.

30. Bryan R. Roberts, "Protestant Groups and Coping with Urban Life in Guatemala," *American Journal of Sociology* 6 (May 1968): 766.

31. Green, "Shifting Affiliations," 173.

32. Green, "Shifting Affiliations," 175.

33. In addition to works by Brusco, Burdick, Green, Kolbenschlag, and Roberts cited above, and Sheldon Annis's work on Protestant economic advancement discussed below, see David Clawson, "Religious Allegiance and Economic Development in Rural Latin America," *Journal of Interamerican Studies and World Affairs* 26 (November 1984): 499–524; Liliana R. Goldin, "An Expression of Cultural Change: Invisible Converts to Protestantism among Highland Guatemala Mayas," *Ethnology* 30 (October 1991): 325–338; Conrad L. Kanagy, "The Formation and Development of a Protestant Conversion Movement among the Highland Quichua of Ecuador," *Sociological Analysis* 51 (summer 1990): 205–17; Cecilia Loreto Mariz, *Coping with Poverty: Pentecostals and Christian Base Communities in Brazil* (Philadelphia: Temple University Press, 1994); Blanca Muratorio, "Protestantism and Capitalism Revisited in the Rural Highlands of Ecuador," *Journal of Peasant Studies* 8 (October 1980): 37–60; James D. Sexton, "Protestantism and Modernization in Two Guatemalan Towns," *American Ethnologist* 5 (May 1978): 280–302; Amy L. Sherman, "And Be Ye Transformed: Christian Orthodoxy and Socio-Economic Transformation in Guatemala," (Ph.D. diss., University of Virginia, 1995); Philip W. Thornton, "Resocialization: Roman Catholics Becoming Protestants in Colombia, South America," *Anthropological Quarterly* 57 (January 1984): 28–38; Paul R. Turner, "Religious Conversion and Community Development," *Journal for the Scientific Study of Religion* 18 (September 1979): 252–60; Max Weber, *The Protestant Ethic and the Spirit of Capitalism* (New York: Scribner's, 1958).

34. Dennis Wheeler, Director of PAVA and owner of Doña Luisa's restaurant, interview with author, Antigua, Guatemala, 25 January 1993.

35. Sheldon Annis, *God and Production in a Guatemala Town* (Austin: University of Texas Press, 1987), especially chapters 5 and 6.

36. Annis, *God and Production*, 102–5.

37. Annis, *God and Production,* 126–39.

38. Bishop Eduardo Fuentes, interview with author, Panajachel, Guatemala, 7 July 1990.

39. Gustavo Adolfo Parajon, Executive Director, Comité Evangélico Pro-Ayuda Al Desarrollo (CEPAD), interview with author, Managua, Nicaragua, 12 November 1993.

40. John Hall, Professor of Mission, Seminario Nazarene, interview with author, San José, Costa Rica, 8 July 1993. See one of the few examples of quantitative research on the sharp decline of active Catholics in Brian Froehle, "The Catholic Church and Politics in Venezuela," in Cleary and Stewart-Gambino, *Conflict and Competition*, 11.

41. Daniel H. Levine, "Religion and Politics in Comparative and Historical Perspective," *Comparative Politics* 19, no. 1 (1986): 97.

42. Levine, "Religion and Politics," 106.

43. John Kessler, *500 Años de evangelización en América Latina desde una perspectiva evangélica* (San José, Costa Rica: Departamento de Publicaciónes del Instituto Internaciónal de Evangelización a Fondo, 1992).

44. Enrique Nuncio, interview with author, San Salvador, 19 January 1995.

45. Roy Peterson, Director of External Relations, Summer Institute of Linguistics, interview with author, Guatemala City, Guatemala, 2 November 1993.

46. David Stoll, "'Jesus is Lord of Guatemala': Evangelical Reform in a Death-Squad State," in *Accounting for Fundamentalisms: The Dynamic Character of Movements*, ed. Martin E. Marty and R. Scott Appleby (Illinois: University of Chicago Press, 1994), 119.

47. See Arturo Escobar and Sonia E. Alvarez, eds., *The Making of Social Movements in Latin America: Identity, Strategy, and Democracy* (Boulder, Colo: Westview, 1992); and Williams, "Movement Dynamics," 785–834.

48. Williams, "Movement Dynamics," 807.

49. Benjamín Cortés, Secretary General, *Centro InterEclesial de Estudios Teológicos y Sociales (CIEETS),* interview with author, Managua, Nicaragua, 12 November 1993.

50. Tarrow, *Power in Movement*, 5.

Chapter Four

Catholic-Protestant Competition in Central America

Something is happening in Latin America that is so overpowering that all structures of the society as well as the value system of the various cultures of Latin America will all be changed by it. This 'something' is an Evangelical revival.

> — Mike Berg and Paul Pretiz
> *The Gospel People* (Miami, Fla.:
> Latin America Mission, 1992)

The statement above reflects the current confident attitude of evangelicals who finally consider themselves ascendant in Latin America. Certainly Protestant missionaries have claimed such ascendance before, particularly at the turn of the century, but this time, as we have seen, more evidence exists to support their claim. Their confidence is a direct challenge to the historically dominant Roman Catholic Church, and it is a challenge that is not going unanswered. One can sense the response of the Catholic Church in pronouncements by the Council of Latin American Bishops, in the proliferation of charismatic Catholic churches; and in the signs that appear now in many residential windows in Central America stating *Somos Catolicos*, meaning in essence, "We are Catholics. No solicitation by Protestants desired." It is clear that numerous families and communities in Latin America have been bitterly divided over religion, whereas other Catholic and Protestant adherents have found ways to coexist peacefully. Furthermore, generalizations about religious tension in one Central American nation may not apply at all to another. Which cultural, political, and theological factors explain the various responses? As the Catholic monopoly breaks down into a marketplace, how can the worst hostilities between the religious rivals be avoided?

69

We will attempt to answer these questions by examining the various forms of "sustained interaction with elites, opponents, and authorities," interaction that Sidney Tarrow identifies as essential to an authentic social movement.[1] This chapter will identify the most prevalent categories of interaction among Catholics and Protestants in Central America. These categories, presented in the form of an "ideal-type" typology, are confrontation, compromise, and cooperation. Competition, whether it is friendly or hostile, is implicit in all three types.

As we pointed out in chapter 3, an important element that Protestants hold in common, despite their diversity, is an emphasis on a personal relationship with Christ, rather than a relationship mediated by clerics or saints. It is this theme that puts Protestants most at odds with Catholics and leads some Pentecostals even to discount Catholics as Christians. However, doctrinal statements by Protestant groups regarding Roman Catholicism are rare, and when such statements do exist, they may have little meaning to the diverse membership. We have already addressed declining denominationalism among the Protestants, and nondenominational agencies are more interested in particular missionary approaches than in specific doctrinal positions.

Reinforcing the weakness of Protestant doctrine and creeds is the lack of seminary training required common among the evangelical pastors who are opening storefront churches throughout Latin America. In such a decentralized, personalistic system it is virtually impossible to know exactly what attitudes and teachings about Catholics are being propounded at the grassroots level. Looking for a shortcut, analysts often oversimplify the Protestant attitude toward Catholics as confrontational. This oversimplification misses many variations. For example, some Protestant groupings have shared liberation theology's priorities for social mission since the 1960s. However, this theology has been much more visible in the Catholic Church which has the centralized voice of the Latin American Bishop's conferences (CELAM conferences). In our analysis we shall attempt to find the middle ground between oversimplifying assumptions and incomprehensible diversity. Before addressing typology of Catholic-Protestant interaction, we will describe briefly the institution that the evangelicals are facing.

THE ROMAN CATHOLIC CHURCH
IN CENTRAL AMERICA

Although the Catholic Church is not nearly as fragmented as Protestantism, that divisions that do exist are extremely important because unity under the pope is generally seen as central to the definition of Catholicism. However, in Latin America this linkage was always weak because historically Catholics were given a great deal of autonomy in the western hemisphere. "Catholic" teachings and practices vary widely, not only from country to country but also in different dioceses. The Latin American bishops have only met as a somewhat unified body (CELAM) four times, and these meetings did not begin until the mid-1950s, the last one occurring in Santo Domingo, Dominican Republic, in October 1992. However, since the 1960s, the dissension in Latin America has been so open and so deep-seated that the Vatican has increasingly intervened, sensing a crisis for the institution.

Perhaps the most dramatic concern facing the Catholic Church in Central America is that a large majority of its members are nominal Catholics who are not active and therefore do not fall into any particular Catholic "category." Furthermore, those Catholics who are active are now internally divided into (1) traditionalists, who maintain close ties to the Vatican and are obedient to its rules; (2) representatives of the "progressive church" who expound various forms of liberation theology; and (3) members of the newest charismatic movement which imitates Pentecostal styles of worship within the Catholic structure. In some areas—particularly in Guatemala with its large Mayan population—*costumbrista* Catholic sects, which incorporate indigenous beliefs, are also identifiable.[2] This splintering of the Church, particularly the evolution of liberation theology, has been analyzed extensively elsewhere and will only be reviewed here in regard to Central American nations.[3] These divisions are important to the present discussion, for their influence on Catholic and Protestant interactions. We shall examine the countries individually first in order to outline the historical/political environment, recognizing that religion in Latin America is highly politicized. We cannot faithfully assess Catholic-Protestant relations without placing the churches in the approximate context of particular political cultures. This outline is admittedly a drastic simplification of complex historical events since our intent here is only to highlight differences among these five neighboring countries.

Costa Rica

In terms of sustaining a stable democracy and a relatively strong economy, Costa Rica has been a fortunate anomaly in Central America (although it is currently experiencing its most serious economic decline in decades). The small nation has also been an anomaly in recent patterns of development for the Roman Catholic Church. Under the strong leadership of the Archbishop of San José, Sanabria Martínez (1940-52), the Church was a force for social reform rather than a stronghold of conservatism. However, in the 1960s, when the Church elsewhere in Central America was discovering social activism, the Costa Rican Catholic Church was becoming more quiescent.

The tenure of Archbishop Sanabria illustrates how effective the Church can be in facilitating social and economic change when its goals coincide with the goals of the government. Sanabria and President Rafael Angel Calderón Guardia both assumed their leadership roles in 1940, and both men were committed to Catholic social doctrine.[4] The new president implemented a package of socioeconomic legislation on behalf of workers, including a social security system and legal guarantees for labor unions. Sanabria and the bishops issued declarations in full support of the president's agenda. In addition, the leaders of the Communist party agreed to end their antireligious rhetoric for the sake of forming a productive coalition with the government and the Church. At that point in time the United States government was in alliance with the Soviet Union against the Axis powers and did not hinder the Costa Rican reforms. Thus, religious and political forces, both national and international, coalesced for a brief period of history. Political scientist Philip J. Williams asserts that "[i]t was probably the success of the social reforms which spared Costa Rica much of the brutal repression characteristic of its Central American neighbours."[5]

In the 1950s the political pendulum began to swing away from welfare statest reform, just as it did in the United States and elsewhere as the global economy recovered from the Depression era. Furthermore, Sanabria's successors as archbishop followed the general philosophy that the Church should stick to spiritual matters and avoid socioeconomic positions. By 1968, at the historic Medellín Conference of Bishops, the Costa Rican Archbishop Rodriguez Quiros refused to sign documents that declared a "preferential option for the poor." Instead he endorsed the Costa Rican socioeconomic system and refused even to debate political mobilization of the poor.

It was not until 1979 that the national Church hierarchy finally issued a pastoral letter addressing political and economic matters. The letter responded to crisis conditions in Costa Rica that were caused by extreme dependency on foreign capital, indebtedness, inflation, and unemployment.[6] In the 1980s the Catholic Church was politically cooperative with the administrations of presidents Luis Alberto Monge (1982-86) and Oscar Arnulfo Arias (1986-90), particularly favoring the Arias peace plan for the region during his tenure. In response to the conservative government of Rafael Angel Calderón (1990-94) the Costa Rican Catholic hierarchy published several statements on poverty, landlessness, and abuse of workers. In general, the Catholic Church in Costa Rica has tended to act in the manner of a diligent liberal interest group—critical, but not revolutionary. Members of the small Christian base community movement in Costa Rica often express frustration that the Church is not more radical.[7]

Interestingly, this nonconflictual, centrist Catholic Church has also been the Church in Central America least vulnerable to the Protestant movement, as we saw in chapter 2. This resistance is not due to a lack of effort by evangelical missionaries, since Costa Rica is the most "overreached" nation in Central America, i.e., many missionaries go there to convert a fairly small number of "nonbelievers."[8] The Costa Rican example indicates that the economic/political context is a key factor influencing the success of Protestant evangelism and subsequent tension with the Catholic Church. Aggressive proselytizing by missionaries is not the most vital factor in the Protestant movement. Cultural realignments, divided elite opposition, and widening opportunities are more important for the development of a social movement. These forces are at work in Costa Rica, but not to the same extent as in other Central American nations.

El Salvador

Catholicism in El Salvador has been far more politicized than in Costa Rica—and more strongly influenced by liberation theology, after centuries of status quo conservatism. The political culture of El Salvador has been influenced by extreme poverty, uprisings, repression, and intense anticommunism. A seminal event occurred in 1932, when a *campesino* uprising led by Farabundo Martí, a communist, was brutally suppressed by Gen. Maximiliano Hernández Martínez. Ten to thirty thousand Salvadorans were killed in the rebellion. Instead of inspiring reforms for the poor, the 1932 slaughter served as justification for a powerful, virtually autonomous military in El Salvador to stamp out any hint of "communist" organizing.[9] In the 1960s and 1970s, however, both secular and religious activism increased in El Salvador. The activists were mobilized by cruel inequities in the country and encouraged by the Medellín conference, which had endorsed liberation theology. Catholic and Protestant missionaries plus many laypeople became involved in human rights, workers' rights, and land reform issues. The Catholic movement of Christian Democrats was mobilized into a powerful political party (PDC). Jesuit priests in some areas began organizing increasing numbers of Christian base communities. Many church leaders openly joined the revolutionary *Frente Farabundo Martí Para la Liberación Nacional* (FMLN) during the course of the twelve-year civil war (1980-92).

The predictable response of the military was to target the churches for hundreds of attacks, particularly during 1980 and 1981 when the military's strategy toward civilians was the most ruthless. This targeting often had no substantive military rationale. Neutral civilians, Protestant and Catholic, were slaughtered by the military, as at El Mozote, where over eight hundred Salvadorans, primarily women and children, primarily Protestants, were massacred.[10] In 1980 Archbishop Oscar Arnulfo Romero was assassinated by the military as he was saying mass, and later that year four female Catholic missionaries from the United States were raped and murdered. As recently as 1989, six Jesuit priests, their housekeeper, and her daughter were killed at the Universidad Centroamericana José Simeon Cañas (UCA). The numerous religious martyrs in El Salvador continue to inspire the poor, particularly within the popular church.

Romero's successor, Archbishop Arturo Rivera y Damas, was regarded as being neutral enough in the struggle to serve as a mediator in the periodic peace talks between the government and the FMLN, but his neutrality did not mean quiescence. Rivera y Damas consistently lobbied the U.S. government to end its support of the Salvadoran military.[11] He also helped organize a national debate in 1988 in which dozens of civic organizations pressed for peace, demilitarization, and political pluralism. Nevertheless, the following year, Alfredo Cristiani and the rightist ARENA party achieved electoral victory. Some analysts explain this as a sign of opposition to corruption in the Christian Democratic Party under President Duarte. The FMLN refused to participate in the election in any way because FMLN leaders doubted the validity of the electoral process.[12]

The intervention of the United Nations in the peace process contributed to the signing of peace accords in December 1992. As part of the peace accords, both the government and the FMLN agreed to the creation of an independent ad hoc commission and a truth commission whose task it was to investigate human rights violations during the war. The parties also agreed to host a team of almost eight hundred United Nations observers and staff (ONUSAL). The hope was that investigations by the Ad Hoc Commission and the Truth Commission would push the government to rein in the military and move toward democracy and economic reform. As a U.N. spokesperson noted, "A new mentality toward Salvadoran authority must be developed—people must learn that human rights violations won't come from figures of authority."[13]

The Truth Commission report issued in March 1993 blamed 85 percent of the twenty-two thousand human rights violations on the military and on right-wing paramilitary death squads. These violations included Archbishop Romero's murder, the El Mozote massacre, and the 1989 murders at the Universidad Centroamericana.[14] International pressure on President Cristiani then increased to remove nineteen military officers who had not already resigned, retired, or been reassigned. By the end of June 1993 these officers were removed; however, the National Assembly voted amnesty for them, an amnesty that was supported by some leaders of the FMLN because the Truth Commission had also cited the FMLN for human rights atrocities. The peace accords were severely undermined by over two dozen political assassinations in 1993 that were apparently aimed at disrupting the 1994 elections. The Salvadoran military death squads are blamed for most of these deaths.[15] Thus human rights atrocities still appear to be coming from "figures of authority." Presidential candidate Ruben Zamora once noted that the only institutions the people *do* trust in El Salvador are "the NGOs [non-government organizations] and the Church."[16]

Thus the Church played a highly visible role before and during the violence and gave the peace initiative credibility. However, the positions taken by leaders of the Salvadoran Catholic Church are evolving. Official statements made by the Salvadoran conference of bishops have been critical of their government and the U.S. government, as well as the FMLN and their international supporters. Other prelates have sought to depoliticize the Church in El Salvador altogether. They are using a two-pronged strategy that (1) encourages growth of the conservative charismatic Catholic groups and reduces institutional support for the Christian base communities; and (2) provides the displaced and refugee community with vital humanitarian and development aid, especially through the archdiocesan Social Secretariat.[17]

Meanwhile, the evangelicals have made dramatic inroads in the country (as always, the figures regarding growth are rough estimates):

> Nowhere else in Central America has the increase of evangelical churches been so fast and dramatic. Of all the evangelical missions and churches founded in El Salvador, nearly 50 percent have opened in the past ten years. Since 1978, the annual rate of growth has ranged from 15 to 22 percent. . . . The country has over 3,300 evangelical churches operated by some 79 evangelical denominations and sects.[18]

Survey data indicate that Protestant growth in El Salvador has been most intense among the poorest and least educated strata. The surveys also show that the Protestants do not particularly support the right-wing ARENA party nor the remnant guerrilla presence. Rather, the tragic upheaval of civil war and the widening opportunities brought by peace contribute to the evangelical movement as an apparent "survival strategy" on many levels.[19]

Honduras

The social activism of the Catholic Church in Honduras actually predates the emphasis given by the 1968 conference at Medellín. However, rather than focusing on establishing base communities, many members of the Honduran Church joined in the Social Christian movement in the early 1960s. This movement was instigated by both the Church and the reformist government of Villeda Morales (1957-63) in order to head off communist organizing in the country. Numerous educational organizations, *campesino* associations, and unions were formed in the name of development. The movement was consolidated by the formation of an umbrella group called CONCORDE (Coordinating Council for Development), which included several Church organizations such as Catholic Relief Services and Caritas.[20]

At first the goals of the Social Christian efforts were fairly modest and dealt with improving living conditions through education and technical assistance. Gradually some clergy and *campesino* leaders began broadening their goals to include deeper systemic change for Honduras. As some organizations became more militant and political, the enthusiasm of the institutional Catholic Church waned. The Church hierarchy formally withdrew from CONCORDE in 1971, showing its preference to work for reforms within the confines of the existing power structure.

In 1975 the forces of the status quo and the emergent popular church of Social Christians tragically collided in the department of Olancho. Twelve *campesino* activists and two priests were killed in disputes with the large landowners. Many foreign priests were expelled or arrested, and critical Catholic radio stations and *campesino* centers were closed. The hierarchical church reacted immediately by denouncing the Olancho repression, but it also reduced support for socially active lay groups. Taking defensive action similar to moves by the Church in El Salvador, some members of the Honduran Catholic hierarchy shifted their support to the less political Charismatic Renewal Movement. Others asserted loyalty to the traditional Church.[21]

In the 1980s the Reagan administration used Honduras as a training ground for Nicaraguan contras; the country was also drawn into civil wars in El Salvador and Guatemala. During this time the Church in Honduras recovered its voice against repression somewhat in response to the violence that spilled over from neighboring countries. When the Honduran military persecuted refugees from El Salvador and Guatemala, the diocese of Santa Rosa de Cópan protested and formed a Refugee Committee to assist war refugees. Human rights concern was also evidenced in the Church's formation of the Christian Movement for Justice.[22] The Honduran Catholic bishops demanded that a truth commission similar to the one in El Salvador investigate human rights violations in Honduras.[23] They have strongly criticized not only the conservative Callejas government but also the business community and the electoral process in the country. Their criticism undoubtedly contributed to Carlos Alberto Reina's 1993 defeat of Callejas's designated successor.

As elsewhere in Latin America, a major internal weakness of the Catholic Church in Honduras is its dependency on foreign clergy and funding. Of approximately 280 priests working in the country, about 220 are foreigners. When outspoken priests are foreign, it is relatively easy for the military to deport them or intimidate them into leaving Honduras.[24] This fact makes the recent pronouncement by bishops of the Honduran Catholic Church particularly courageous. They appealed to military officers to admit their guilt in the human rights violations of the 1980s, asking them to reveal the location of the "disappeared and detained" and to face trial. Tegucigalpa Archbishop Oscar Rodriguez had supported amnesty for the offenders, but apparently he could not convince the other bishops to be so forgetful.[25] The Honduran Catholic Church is now a diverse community and institution. But it is severely understaffed, and people are moving to Protestantism in growing numbers.

Guatemala

The Catholic Church in Guatemala is almost as understaffed as its counterpart in Honduras—two-thirds of its clergy are foreigners.[26] Until recently the theological and political leanings of Church leaders have ranged from moderately conservative to extremely conservative, although prophetic, reformist voices always seemed to ring out in particular dioceses. The perception of conservatism can be largely explained by the dominance in the Guatemalan Church of two leaders: Archbishop Mariano Rossell (1939-63) and Archbishop Mario Casariego (1964-83). Mariano Rossell was a virulent anticommunist who cooperated with the U.S. CIA to help overthrow the government of Jacobo Arbenz in 1954, which opened the way for over thirty years of military dictatorships in Guatemala. After the fall or Arbenz, Rossell sent his congratulations to the new military government:

> I send you warm greetings and fervent congratulations in the name of the nation which awaits you with open arms, recognizing and admiring your sincere patriotism. May our Lord God guide you and your heroic companions in your liberating campaign against atheistic communism.[27]

The military governments in the 1950s and early 1960s rewarded Mariano Rossell's Church by building new cathedrals and schools and encouraging an influx of priests and nuns from Franco's Spain and the United States.

Archbishop Casariego continued the reciprocal relationship between the Church, the military, and the wealthy. In the wake of Vatican II and Medellín, however, Guatemalan bishops began to speak more forcefully against repression and on behalf of the poor. They also organized the National Bishops Conference in 1964, which provided a larger forum for positions contrary to the Archbishop's, positions that encouraged some social activism at the local church level. The by now familiar response to a more visibly progressive church was military terrorism. In 1980 and 1981 six priests and dozens of lay workers were assassinated.[28] Meanwhile, Casariego supported the standard charity programs for the poor, mostly through the Caritas organization. He was consistently identified more as an ally of the military than of the poor until his death in 1983.

As the guerrilla war intensified and as economic inequities and human rights violations increased, the activism of many Guatemalan priests and nuns became more prominent. For example, Padre Andrés Girón led a massive march on the capital in 1986 for land reform, winning the sale of some land to *campesinos* and a few other concessions from the Cerezo government. In 1988 the bishops became more assertive, directly referring to the explosive problem of land tenure in the pastoral letter, "The Clamor for Land." In addition, the new Archbishop, Prospero Penados del Barrio, has been much more a critic of the government than his predecessors. For instance, in 1995 he fully supported the Guatemalan bishops' project to investigate and analyze over thirty years of political violence in Guatemala. This project arose out of the Church's frustration with the U.N.-mediated Truth Commission for Guatemala, which would not be allowed to "name names" and would only begin its task after the long-awaited peace treaty was finally signed. The Catholic "alternate truth commission" will apparently pursue in-depth investigation, will name violators, and will be backed by the credibility of the Church.[29]

Thus the Guatemalan Catholic Church has changed since the days of Casariego, and the appointment of Penados del Barrio is an interesting exception to the many conservative appointments John Paul II has made.[30] However, the case of Padre Girón illustrates that the Church is far from unified. Girón was strongly criticized by the Vatican for his political activities, but he continued to have the support of Archbishop Penados del Barrio. Nevertheless, when Girón was elected to the Guatemalan Congress in 1990, his presiding bishop removed him from authority in his parish churches, leaving Girón's ecclesial status in limbo.[31] Canonical regulations mandate that priests cannot publicly exercise religious functions and at the same time hold public office, an issue that also arose in Nicaragua. The Church is concerned to prevent individuals from using religious status to legitimize political careers. The rationale behind official Catholic positions may be complex and nuanced, as in the case of Padre Girón; nevertheless, the public perception is often confused by apparently conflicting messages from the Church.

The Church is in an extremely difficult position vis-à-vis the Protestants in Guatemala. Many wealthier Catholics have felt betrayed by liberation theology, and some have moved to neo-Pentecostal churches. The poor majority, on the other hand, are attracted to Pentecostal churches for more positive answers to their suffering than Catholicism offers.[32]

Nicaragua

The Catholic Church in Nicaragua has been the most polarized Church in the region. On the one side have been the CEBs and liberation theology advocates who, in general, support the redistributive goals of the Sandinistas; on the other, traditional, side has been Cardinal Obando y Bravo. The division crosses generational, class, and geographical lines. The polarization has been aggravated by the cooperation that has occurred between the Sandinistas (FSLN) and the Protestants (discussed below) which infuriated many in the Roman Catholic hierarchy. Thus, the Church must decide what its proper role in politics is, and also whether "Marxists" (i.e., Sandinistas) can remain Christian.[33]

During the last thirty years each side of the Catholic divide has attempted reconciliation with the other side. For instance, the hierarchical Church actually supported the formation of Christian base communities in the 1970s and 1980s, and Obando y Bravo and other leaders spoke out against the ruthless Somoza dictatorship, particularly after Somoza's callous response to the 1972 earthquake. When the Sandinista guerrillas finally succeeded in overthrowing Somoza in 1979, the Nicaraguan bishops gave a qualified endorsement to the new government. Some bishops, however, remained openly opposed and, in any case, the Sandinistas were not eager to relinquish any of their hard-won power to former opponents in the Church. As early as 1983-84 the papal nuncio and charge in Nicaragua were urging local bishops to defuse tensions with the Sandinistas. But the intensity of the war with the contras caused each side to harden its position, making compromise difficult for the polarized church.[34]

The depth of the fissure was revealed when some members of the Catholic Church hierarchy who had most loudly criticized the government (including Bishop Vega) were expelled from Nicaragua in 1985. The Sandinista government also censored the critical Catholic periodical, *Iglesia*.[35] The popular Church, which had prospered in the period leading up to the 1979 triumph, now declined in the years of the revolution at the direction of the Church hierarchy. For instance, in the Managua archdiocese, authorities removed many priests who had been working with CEBs; in the activist diocese of Esteli, at least twenty priests were removed by the bishop between 1983 and 1987.[36] The Church also entered into a lengthy dispute with four priests who refused to resign from their seats in the revolutionary government as the Catholic hierarchy had demanded: Fernando Cardenal, former minister of education, Ernesto Cardenal, former minister of culture, Miguel D'Escoto, former foreign minister, and Edgard Parrales, former minister of social welfare (who eventually left the priesthood altogether).[37]

By 1987, in the spirit of the Esquipulas II peace accord, President Ortega eased censorship and allowed the exiled Catholic leaders to return. Cardinal Obando y Bravo even chaired the National Reconciliation Commission to hammer out the details of the peace agreement, which the Sandinistas ultimately signed. In 1990 Violetta Chamorro was elected president, and her UNO party won fifty-one seats out of ninety-three in the National Assembly, with the clear assistance of Cardinal Obando and other bishops of the traditional Church. The Sandinistas won thirty-nine seats and thus stepped down to the role of the opposition.[38] As for the Catholic Church in this new arrangement, conservatives in the Latin American Bishops Conference (CELAM) continued a campaign to discredit the progressive Church in Nicaragua. Responses have included the relocation of priests, press and broadcast propaganda and support for charismatic Catholicism, which is a popular imitation of evangelicalism.[39] Furthermore, the Chamorro administration has rewarded the traditional Church leaders with a new Catholic cathedral in Managua, Catholic University facilities, and the appointment of Cardinal Obando's associates to the Ministry of Education. As Minister of Education, Humberto Belli has the authority to direct curriculum in Nicaragua, which some critics have seen as a step to state sponsorship of Roman Catholicism.[40]

Ironically, one reason the network of Christian base communities diminished during the war is that their members were most likely to become active in the revolution. "The most educated people went off to the government ministries, while the kids joined the army," one base community leader concluded.[41] Another reason for decline is that the base communities in their drive for systemic change were simply not meeting the spiritual and emotional needs of many Nicaraguans. Still, in certain areas of Nicaragua, numerous base communities continue practicing liberation theology. One Episcopalian priest working in the area of Matagalpa observes that the members of these Catholic base communities "operate anyway, nonconflictually but nonrecognized [by the hierarchy]. These people are not leaving the Church yet, as in the Reformation, but I don't know how much longer they will hang on."[42]

The Catholic Church in Nicaragua has been severely weakened by its polarizing politicization. Catholic scholar Penny Lernoux argued in her book *People of God* that the base community movement was a source of renewal for the Catholic Church; however, most members of the Church hierarchy treated the popular church as a threat to centralized authority. In the 1990s they have seized opportunities provided by the election of a devout Catholic, Violetta Chamorro, to secure their position of centralized leadership once again. One church historian in Nicaragua stated that "the Catholic Church's policy in the next fifty years is a restoration of its power."[43]

The latest episode in this stormy marriage between church and state is a series of bombings of Catholic churches in Nicaragua—fifteen small blasts between May and October 1995. It is speculated that the bombings, which have caused only minor damage, are an attempt by the Sandinistas to destabilize the October 1996 elections and that they may be a prelude to a violent campaign season.[44] That political motivations would be attributed automatically to this religious vandalism certainly is evidence of the intense politicization of the Church. It is no wonder that the battles have left many Nicaraguans deeply disillusioned by Catholicism overall and have provided a wide opening in the country for the *evangelicos*. As we will see below, the growing, widely-respected evangelical sector in Nicaragua defies the common scholarly perception of Protestants as apolitical. In Nicaragua it is difficult for any church to remain detached from politics.

Summary

We have seen that after centuries of generally reinforcing the oligarchical status quo, the Roman Catholic Church in the last three decades responded to the priorities of Vatican II and liberation theology. But social science observers have exaggerated the degree of influence that these priorities exerted on the internal structures of the Church and on the people.[45] The need to engage the Church in systemic change on behalf of the poor was most forcefully pronounced at the 1968 Conference of Latin American Bishops (CELAM is the Spanish acronym) at Medellín and again in Puebla at the 1979 Conference of Latin American Bishops. However, the Catholic hierarchy has been ambivalent at best toward liberation theology, and at times, in the case of Nicaragua, has actively opposed it. Thus the progressive, populist shift of the Catholic Church has both reinvigorated a stagnant institution *and* produced dissent and confusion.

The results of the fourth bishops' conference (CELAM) at Santo Domingo in 1992 illustrate this confusion. Vatican representatives at the conference attempted to insert their positions into the documents, while also allowing the bishops their traditional autonomy from Rome. For instance, the Vatican saw that the word "liberation" was changed to the more benign "reconciliation," but sustained the church's "option for the poor."[46] The church hierarchy also dealt with the problematic CEBs and the newer charismatic groups. Santo Domingo documents called for more unity and coordination of the CEBs among the local pastors and their bishops, a stance that could affect the spontaneous identity of the CEBs. Similarly, the charismatic groups were vaguely instructed to be less fundamentalist, less charismatic, and less exclusive.[47]

Obviously the Church hierarchy is struggling with the larger identity of an ancient institution that is experiencing tremendous change. Despite the popular perception of an all-powerful Latin American Catholicism, the Church is divided, understaffed, financially weak, and on the defensive. Catholic theologian Enrique Dussel (who is himself controversial) describes the essence of this difficult defensive position [the word "sect" is the somewhat derogatory term Catholics generally use for Protestant churches]:

According to Rome, the threat posed by Protestantism is a serious one. A huge sector of the population that is poor and marginalized will be Protestant by the end of the century. In 10 to 15 years, more than 40 percent of Latin Americans will be Protestant. Rome blames liberation theologians, claiming they have concentrated on political instead of spiritual matters. According to the hierarchy, people have turned to sects out of their need for spiritual expression. For me, it's the opposite. The Vatican is in fact responsible for the people's turning to spiritual communities, even if they discourage participation in politics, are irresponsible and focus on individual salvation—like the fundamentalist sects—because the Vatican has no grassroots ministry. Sects offer the people a community. People know each other by name and the pastor is personally interested in them.[48]

THE CATHOLIC-PROTESTANT RELATIONSHIP

Confrontation

Dussel's statement (above) indicates a grudging admiration by Catholics for some aspects of the evangelical movement in Latin America. The statement also indicates an intense sense of competition with them as well as frustration that the Vatican is not rising to the challenge in the way Dussel and others think it should. Penny Lernoux, for example, expressed a similar frustration with the hierarchy:

> [The CEBs] offer many of the same things that attract the poor to the [fundamentalists], including a more personalized religious environment, solidarity, and a sense of equality. . . . [B]ecause Rome feared the loss of its institutional power to a democratic base it discouraged the growth of the communities. The Curia could not see that it was aiding Catholicism's avowed enemies in the fundamentalist churches by opposing a lay-directed renewal.[49]

Pope John Paul II, as these Catholic critics observe, appears to be stepping into this confrontation in the armor of traditionalism. More conservative bishops have been appointed throughout Latin America in recent years. The progressive CEBs persist nevertheless, as well as CEBs that are more traditional-oriented. Therefore, at Santo Domingo the hierarchy proposed drawing them more closely into the structure of the institutional church. On the other hand, the entire claim that the Catholic losses are attributable to lack of support for liberation theology CEBs may be "disingenuous," as Jean Daudlin and W. E. Hewitt point out. They note that "[t]he progressives delivered no more faithful, no more seminarians, no more priests than their more traditionalist counterparts."[50] The weaknesses in the Roman Catholic Church are more fundamental than liberation theology could, or can, correct.

In terms of theology the Vatican is taking a variety of approaches, adding to the overall confusion. At times, the hierarchy appears willing to compromise, as we shall see below. But at other times the theological stance is clearly confrontational, as in the New Universal Catechism, which is the most strictly doctrinal document issued by Rome since before Vatican II. As theologian Fernando Castillo explains, the basis for the Universal Catechism "is the idea that the Catholic Church is the one true church and the only true Christians are Catholics."[51] Unless it is widely disseminated and read, the primary significance of the new catechism may be symbolic—symbolic of a confrontational approach in the religious showdown with Protestants. It has always been true that Roman Catholicism officially taught the exclusiveness of its Christianity. However, because the early Protestant missionaries in Latin America were so culturally inconsequential in the past, they were largely ignored except in papers perennially published by the bishops that denounced the sects. The Roman Catholic Church hierarchy now points to the evangelicals as their most serious challenge. Pope John Paul II made it clear in Santo Domingo that the official position of the Church toward evangelicals would be confrontational—he urged the bishops to defend their flocks against the "rapacious wolves."[52]

As for the evangelicals, initial observation leads to the conclusion that the majority are similarly confrontational in their theology. However, in view of the fragmentation and local diversity that are characteristic of Protestantism, the idea of an "official position" is meaningless. Nevertheless, it is clear that Catholic religious distinctives are sinful idolatry to many fundamentalist Protestants, such as devotion to the Virgin Mary, sainthood, and submission to the pope and bishops.

The theological differences are enhanced by the tendency of any kind of fundamentalism to practice "moral dualism," i.e., "a view of the world as sharply divided between embattled camps of good and evil—in which fundamentalists see themselves as a divinely called group."[53] Conversations with dozens of evangelical converts in Central America revealed to me that the common opinion about Catholic friends and family members is that they are unsaved and not Christian. Another commonly held opinion about Catholics is that they encourage a low moral standard, particularly in regard to alcohol and sexuality.

Thus the religious battle lines appear to be sharply drawn. Militant terminology that evokes scenes of violence is, unfortunately, appropriate in some cases. For instance, in Guatemala religious riots have occurred. In August 1991 more than seventy people were wounded in front of a Guatemalan cathedral during a riot between traditional Catholics and charismatic believers.[54] The exclusive positions taken by both sides in this confrontational approach, of one denying the Christianity (and salvation) of the other, have been extremely painful for numerous families and divisive for communities. One community leader in Guatemala dramatically assessed the situation: "The two most sensitive issues in Guatemala, which are never discussed but are in the back of everyone's minds, are racism [between ladinos and indigenous Mayans] and now the fear of religious war."[55]

Although confrontation between evangelicals and Catholics is nothing new, events that have occurred recently in Central America illustrate how divided the Catholic Church often has been. Even when the pope has been most critical of liberation theology, for example, some Latin American bishops and their allies within the curia have openly disagreed with him. The Vatican secretary of state, Casaroli, has been active in moderating positions of some conservatives in the Vatican and in Central America. Just as Protestant fragmentation has often been exaggerated by observers, so has Catholic unity. Thus it would be completely misleading to end a discussion assessing Protestant-Catholic relations with "confrontation," when the situation is actually complex and dynamic.

Compromise

A less common, but more peaceful, approach to the religious rivalry is for Protestants to be more accepting of Catholics as

Christians, and for the Catholic Church to accept an evangelical style of worship and some of its theological substance. This approach to Catholicism is practiced by missionary agencies and missionaries who are sensitive to the cultural importance of being Catholic in Latin America. They assert that "God is at work *within* the Catholic Church," and they cite a variety of evidence.

For instance, the charismatic movement among Catholics in Central America is the most vital segment of the Church (although much less so in Nicaragua, where it is a smaller phenomenon associated with the middle class). The charismatic groups, in the manner of Pentecostals, hold prayer meetings and healing campaigns and emphasize personal receiving of the Holy Spirit. In addition, the Catholic Church has encouraged a new "Christian Family" movement, featuring weekend retreats that fortify the home, in the manner of the evangelical emphasis on the family. There is a concentrated effort to distribute the Bible and to encourage study groups. The Bible Society in Latin America currently sells more Bibles to Roman Catholics than to evangelicals.[56]

It is not that Roman Catholics were unconcerned with Bible study or family values in the past. But now the Church is making a creative effort to reach parishioners through these lay ministries—largely in response to the rivalry with evangelicals.[57] Some Protestant missionaries are taking the position that if the Catholic Church can adapt its practices and teachings from within, then they have met their mission goal, regardless of whether these Catholics officially convert to Protestantism. A book disseminated by the prominent mission organization, World Vision emphasizes theological similarities with Catholics, rather than differences:

> There is a broad area of convergence between Catholic teaching and the philosophy of ministry embraced by a number of evangelical development agencies. Such an approach features the centrality of the kingdom of God, God's special concern for the poor and the challenge of world evangelization. . . . [A]ffirmation of a common call to share in Christ's mission in the world is not dependent on uniformity in all points of doctrine and liturgical practice. Among the important areas on which there is essential agreement are: a trinitarian understanding of God, Christology, and the belief that Scriptures provide the primary resource for forming Christians in their faith and shaping their value system.[58]

World Vision also points to the renewed Catholic emphasis on evangelization, such as the "Evangelization 2000" program centered in Rome, not as a threat, but as a positive development for Christianity.[59]

But this spirit of compromise, most often espoused by evangelical scholars and leaders, remains a minority view among the evangelical *members*, and is not accepted by most missionaries. As one Nazarene seminary professor explained, "Too many missionaries are often more anti-Catholic than pro-Gospel, and end up working for a denomination, not Christ."[60] Those attending missionary seminars on this subject in Costa Rica were by and large highly suspicious and at times resentful of the imitative charismatic Catholics.

For their part, some segments of the Catholic Church hierarchy assert that this kind of adaptation is an appropriate response to the Protestant challenge. We have already seen that in El Salvador and Honduras the Vatican supported charismatic groups in the Church as a less political and less controversial alternative to liberation theology. Such willingness to be adaptable has a long history in the Catholic Church under the label of "syncretism." In early colonial days, if conquest of the indigenous peoples did not succeed, Catholic priests were encouraged to adopt every possible aspect of the native religions that would facilitate conversion. Syncretism often resulted in a "folk religion" that incorporated ancient rituals and spiritism into Catholic teachings. In Central America folk Catholicism is most evident in Guatemala among the *cofradía* organizations, which practice a mixture of Mayan customs and Catholic rituals.[61] To a degree, this kind of adaptability is demonstrated today in relation to the charismatic practices, in a "new syncretism."

However, in a theological sense, Church officials are ambivalent about adaptations. When are they acceptable and when do they undermine the essence of Catholicism? The Pope sought more control over the charismatic movement by moving the World Catholic Charismatic Headquarters from Belgium to the Vatican. He also appointed "shepherd" coordinators for different countries to direct the local movement. The charismatic meetings and crusades were instructed not to allow Protestant speakers and to demonstrate loyalty to Catholic doctrines by singing songs to Mary and the saints.[62] Ironically the Vatican response to charismatic groups is similar to its response to Christian base communities—initial support, developing ambivalence, and attempts to reassert control.

Perhaps the following statement best summarizes our description of typologies thus far from an evangelical missionary's perspective:

> I sure do believe that Catholics are Christian. I believe that within that structure they *can* be Christians. After all, they have the same Christ, the same morality standard. But if you ask a native convert, they'll most likely say that Catholics are not Christian. People may be coming out of the Catholic Church after thirty years, and they're angry at Catholicism. For whatever reason, they feel that the priest let them down. But the World is so perverted, it's going to force us to get along eventually![63]

Cooperation

This category of interaction between Catholics and Protestants in Central America is far removed from confrontation. A minority of Protestants, primarily from the traditional or "mainline" churches, approach Catholics and other Protestants in the spirit of ecumenism, i.e., Christian unity. These ecumenical Protestants—Presbyterians, Methodists, Lutherans, Episcopalians, American Baptists, Mennonites, Quakers, some Pentecostals—often feel a great affinity with Catholic practitioners of liberation theology. Many of them have been active in community development and have taken risks side by side with Catholic priests, nuns, and lay workers. As one Episcopal missionary who worked for many years in Nicaraguan CEBs stated, "It is incidental to those of us collaborating, if we are Protestant or Catholic."[64] Competition between these supportive Catholic and Protestants is friendly and occurs only in the sense that all local churches value new members.

The theology inherent in the cooperation type is a theology of religious pluralism rather than exclusiveness—a sense of mutual respect. Liberation theology accommodates such ecumenical inclusiveness because it flows from *praxis* in working for the poor rather than from an exclusive doctrine. Thus this approach does not involve theological compromise, but acceptance. That explains why one evangelical missionary, who is willing to honor some Catholics as "true Christians," stated that "the word 'ecumenical' is eyebrow-raising for most evangelicals; it brings to mind organizations like the World Council of Churches that are too political and too loose in their reading of Scripture."[65] Let us repeat the defining scriptural directive for liberation theology in Jesus's words in Luke 4:18–19: "The Spirit of the Lord is upon me, because he has anointed me to preach good news to the poor. He has sent me to proclaim release of the captives and recovering of sight to the blind, to set at liberty those who are oppressed, to proclaim the acceptable year of the Lord."

Liberation theology emphases, as delineated in Luke 4, have long been present in some Protestant groupings. However, as noted previously, extreme diversity makes this theology a much less visible strand among Protestants than in the Catholic Church, which has the centralized Church CELAM conferences. The closest parallel organization for Protestants in Latin America is the Latin American Evangelical Conference (*Conferencia Evangelica Latinoamericana*, CELA I, II, and III). However, these conferences can hardly be called representative of the Protestant presence in Latin America. At CELA III in Buenos Aires in 1969 only forty-three churches and ecumenical organizations sent representatives to discuss their growing social consciousness.[66] Another umbrella organization for Protestant churches espousing ecumenism and liberation theology is the Office of Church and Society in Latin America (*Iglesia y Sociedad en América Latina*, ISAL), which was originally sponsored by the World Council of Churches.[67]

In 1978 an important Protestant conference was held in Oaxtepec, Mexico. Catholic liberation theologians were present at the meeting, as well as representatives from 110 evangelical churches and ten ecumenical organizations. The delegates passed resolutions calling for the church to take an "option for the poor," a theme that would be repeated at the Puebla conference of the Catholic bishops. However, one organizational result of the Oaxtepec conference illustrated that the impetus for conflict is at least as strong as the desire for conciliation. Some delegates to the conference formed the Latin American Council of Churches (CLAI, *Consejo Latinoamericano de Iglesias*) to continue their discussions about the progressive role of the churches. Just three years later, the Latin American Evangelical Confraternity (*Confraternidad Evangélica*, CONELA) was founded with the express purpose of counteracting CLAI.[68]

Thus Protestant-Catholic cooperation is sketchy in Central America, demonstrated, for example, in the progressive *Conferencia de Iglesias Evangelicas de Guatemala* (CIEDEG) and in the ecumenical organization, Diaconía, in El Salvador, but not widespread. The cooperative approach is probably most common in Nicaragua because of shared revolutionary experiences. The strength of ecumenism in Nicaragua is somewhat paradoxical, given the outspoken opposition to liberation theology by the Catholic hierarchy in that country. But it is probably safe to say that liberation theology Catholics feel more camaraderie toward the ecumenical Protestants they work with than toward the traditional Catholics they have often worked against.

Two organizations in Nicaragua represent conciliation among all Christians who endeavor to empower the poor majority to "better their material, social, and spiritual resources in order to live more abundant lives."[69] These organizations are the Antonio Valdivieso Ecumenical Center (CAV) and CEPAD, which we have encountered before. Both bodies are directed by Protestant ministers (Gary Campbell, a Presbyterian at CAV and Gustavo Parajon, a Baptist at CEPAD), and both bodies work closely with Catholics toward the goals of reflection, empowerment, and development projects benefiting the poor. Their objective is not religious conversion of Catholics, which would place them in a confrontational stance, nor is it to compromise Catholic practices into a Pentecostal mold. Instead, their primary goals involve *praxis* for the poor and reflection flowing from the experience. Recall that CEPAD was formed by evangelical denominations joining together in response to the devastation of the 1972 earthquake. Today many Roman Catholics are welcome participants in CEPAD's ministries.

On the other hand, both CEPAD and CAV leaders have entered into very public confrontations with the traditional Roman Catholic representatives in Managua, especially former Cardinal Obando y Bravo and Humberto Belli, the minister of education. The debates, however, are only about *religious* rivalry in a peripheral way. Conflict among these religious/political leaders in Nicaragua is centered on differences in political and economic philosophy. Interestingly, as the size and prestige of CEPAD has increased, even Obando y Bravo and Humberto Belli have become more conciliatory toward the organization, which may portend a new relationship.[70]

CONCLUSION

The dynamic relationship between Protestants and Catholics in Latin America is still evolving, but we have identified discernible patterns. Confrontation between the more traditional Catholics and the evangelicals is still the dominant pattern of interaction. The Vatican accuses Protestants of crass manipulation of the people, and many Protestants counter with disdain for Catholic "immorality" and neglect of parishioners. But we have seen that Catholics and Protestants have also responded to each other in more creative patterns of compromise and cooperation. At least three important factors are influencing this dynamic: (1) recognition of the serious Protestant challenge to the Catholic Church by both sides that has heightened tension, (2) differing theological emphases, and (3) the different personalities of particular religious leaders in Central American countries. Recall the dramatic differences that existed in the attitudes held by religious personnel in key positions in Central America. Vatican appointees, in particular, take different approaches toward Protestants and toward the state and will influence their flocks. The shift toward a more "popular" Catholic Church in Guatemala occurred with the arrival of the new archbishop, Prospero Penados del Barrio. His conciliatory approach contrasts sharply with Archbishop Casariego's traditionalism. Similarly, Archbishop Rivera y Damas in El Salvador has been far less confrontational than Obando y Bravo in Nicaragua. The Vatican is well aware of the importance of its personnel choices, as evidenced by its strategy to counteract liberation theology by appointing more traditional bishops in recent years. In the next chapter we will examine the importance of leadership dynamics within Protestantism.

In the broader terms of social movement theory, however, the dynamics at work here are more significant than individual personalities. As Tarrow notes, "[M]ovements are produced . . . when they demonstrate the existence of allies and when they reveal the vulnerability of opponents."[71] Thus when Protestantism began to assert itself more aggressively in Central America in the 1970s and 1980s, it highlighted the weaknesses of the Catholic Church. This in turn enhanced the rate of conversion to Protestantism. It is simply true, in the latter decades of the twentieth century, that the Catholic Church in Central America is vulnerable because of complacency, understaffing, organizational rigidity—and now the reality of a formidable group of rival churches. Thus, after decades of denying the scope of the Protestant movement, even traditional Catholics are realizing that they had best meet the challenge in ways that are more innovative than mere confrontation. In a head-on clash they could lose. This can be seen as a healthy crisis for Catholicism. The role of the church is changing as it faces substantial challenges from secular as well as religious competitors, and the Church is showing signs of revitalization among those who participate in its various efforts. There is more cooperation with the evangelicals, and it is not limited to those who favor ecumenicalism. Cardinal Obando y Bravo of Nicaragua, who once publicly dismissed evangelicals as only 1 or 2 percent of the Nicaraguan population, is now openly meeting with Protestant leaders to discuss national problems.[72] Similarly, the Vatican is struggling to direct the Charismatic Catholic trend on one hand, and liberation theology ecumenism on the other. This tolerance vis-à-vis Protestants is often strategic, given the new reality of a religious marketplace in Latin America.

Can any predictions be hazarded regarding Catholic and Protestant tension in Central America? There may well be more confrontation, including violent clashes, in the short term because religious challenges strike at the soul of any culture and are deeply resisted. However, in the longer term, it appears that Tarrow's general analysis of social movement cycles is being played out in the Protestant movement in Central America. He writes:

> As the cycle widens, movements create opportunities for elites and opposition groups too. Alliances form between participants and challengers and oppositional elites make demands for changes that would have seemed foolhardy earlier. . . . The widening logic of collective action leads to outcomes in the sphere of politics, where the

movements that began the cycle can have less and less influence over its outcomes.[73]

In this chapter we have seen how alliances, adaptations, religious pluralism, and cooperation among groups of Catholics and evangelicals are increasingly in evidence and will likely be more so in the future. Perhaps the most compelling reason for compromise and cooperation is that Catholic confrontation with Protestants is simply counterproductive for the Church. In chapter 5 we will turn to the complex sphere of politics, where indeed, the Protestant movement seems to be moving into collective action where it must share influence with other political players.

NOTES

1. Sidney Tarrow, *Power in Movement: Social Movements, Collective Action and Politics* (New York: Cambridge University Press, 1994), 4.

2. Sheldon Annis, *God and Production in a Guatemalan Town* (Austin: University of Texas Press, 1987), 90.

3. A sample listing of the voluminous social science works in English on liberation theology includes Phillip Berryman, *Liberation Theology: Essential Facts about the Revolutionary Movement in Latin America and Beyond* (New York: Pantheon, 1987); Phillip Berryman, *The Religious Roots of Rebellion: Christians in Central American Revolutions* (Maryknoll, N.Y.: Orbis, 1984); Michael L. Budde, *The Two Churches: Catholicism and Capitalism in the World-System* (Durham: Duke University Press, 1992); Dermot Keogh, ed., *Church and Politics in Latin America* (New York: St. Martin's, 1990); Daniel H. Levine, *Popular Voices in Latin American Catholicism* (Princeton, N.J.: Princeton University Press, 1992); Daniel H. Levine, ed., *Religion and Political Conflict in Latin America* (Chapel Hill: University of North Carolina Press, 1986); Scott Mainwaring, *The Catholic Church and Politics in Brazil, 1916–1985* (Stanford, Calif.: Stanford University Press, 1986); Scott Mainwaring and Alexander Wilde, eds., *The Progressive Church in Latin America* (Indiana: University of Notre Dame Press, 1983); Arthur F. McGovern, *Liberation Theology and Its Critics* (Maryknoll, N.Y.: Orbis, 1989); John R. Pottenger, *The Political Theory of Liberation Theology: Toward a Reconvergence of Social Values and Social Science* (Albany: State University of New York Press, 1986); Paul E. Sigmund, *Liberation Theology at the Crossroads:*

Democracy or Revolution? (New York: Oxford University Press, 1990); and Christian Smith, *The Emergence of Liberation Theology: Radical Religion and Social Movement Theory* (Illinois: University of Chicago Press, 1991).

4. Catholic "social doctrine" is a reference to the Church's response to the material needs of the poor and working classes—a religious and humanitarian response that was also a deliberate counter to Marxist ideology.

5. Philip J. Williams, *The Catholic Church and Politics in Nicaragua and Costa Rica* (Pittsburgh: University of Pittsburgh Press, 1989), 111. Also see Margaret E. Crahan, "Religion and Democratization in Central America," in *Political Parties and Democracy in Central America*, ed. Louis W. Goodman et al. (Boulder, Colo.: Westview, 1992), 332–36.

6. Williams, *Catholic Church and Politics*, 128, 136.

7. Williams, *Catholic Church and Politics*, 122, 136; and regarding Calderon see Crahan, "Religion and Democratization," 336; also author's interviews at the Seminario Biblio Latinoamericano in San Jose, Costa Rica, July 1993.

8. Mission Advanced Research Center, *Mission Handbook, 1993–1995* (Monrovia, Calif.: World Vision Press, 1993) 6.

9. Crahan, "Religion and Democratization," 336.

10. Mark Danner, "The Truth of El Mozote," *The New Yorker*, 6 December 1993, 50–133.

11. Penny Lernoux, *People of God: The Struggle for World Catholicism* (New York: Viking, 1989), 178, 405; and Jorge Caceres Prendes, "Political Radicalization and Popular Pastoral Practices in El Salvador, 1969–1985," in Mainwaring and Wilde, *The Progressive Church*, 137–41.

12. Crahan, "Religion and Democratization," 338; and Cristina Equizabal, "Parties, Programs, and Politics in El Salvador," in Goodman et al., *Political Parties*, 144–48.

13. Public Relations Director, *Observaciónes Nacionales Unidos en Salvador* (ONUSAL), presentation witnessed by author, San Salvador, El Salvador, 20 January 1993.

14. *Latinamerica Press*, 25 March 1993, 1.

15. "U.N. Team Probing New Slayings," *The Miami Herald*, 10 November 1993, 1; anonymous interview with author, San Salvador, El Salvador, 4 November 1993.

16. Ruben Zamora, FDR member, vice president of National Assembly during Cristiani's presidency, interview with author, San Salvador, El Salvador, 19 January 1993.

17. Inter-Hemispheric Education Resource Center, *Private Organi-*

zations with U.S. Connections, Directory and Analysis: El Salvador (Albuquerque: Inter-Hemispheric Education Resource Center, 1988), 4. Satya R. Pattnayak notes that Catholicism in El Salvador is now highly favorable primarily because of the influx of hundreds of Catholic religious personnel other than priests; see Appendix in *Organized Religion in the Political Transformation of Latin America* (Lanham, Md.: University Press of America, 1995) 209–10.

18. Resource Center, *Directory: El Salvador*, 4.

19. Kenneth Coleman et al., "Protestantism in El Salvador: Conventional Wisdom versus the Survey Evidence," in *Rethinking Protestantism in Latin America*, ed. Virginia Garrard-Burnett and David Stoll (Philadelphia: Temple University Press, 1993), 111–42.

20. Inter-Hemispheric Education Resource Center, *Private Organizations with U.S. Connections, Directory and Analysis: Honduras* (Albuquerque: Inter-Hemispheric Education Resource Center, 1988), 4–5. Also see Gustavo Blanco and Jaime Valverde, *Honduras: Iglesia y Cambio Social* (San José, Costa Rica: DEI and Guaymuras, 1990); and Ernesto Paz Aguilar, "The Origin and Development of Political Parties in Honduras," in Goodman et al., *Political Parties and Democracy*, 161–74.

21. Resource Center, *Directory: Honduras*, 5–6.

22. Resource Center, *Directory: Honduras*, 7.

23. *Central America Report*, 17 September 1993.

24. Resource Center, *Directory: Honduras*, 3; Crahan, "Religion and Democratization," 352.

25. "Church Changes Human Rights Stance," *Latinamerica Press*, 8 February 1996.

26. Inter-Hemispheric Education Resource Center, *Directory and Analysis: Private Organizations with U.S. Connections: Guatemala*, (Albuquerque: Inter-Hemispheric Education Resource Center, 1988), 6.

27. Resource Center, *Directory: Guatemala*, 4.

28. Crahan, "Religion and Democratization," 339.

29. Paul Jeffrey, "Telling the Truth: Church Project in Guatemala," in *Christian Century* 30 August–6 September 1995, 804–6; also see *Latinamerica Press*, 11 May 1995, 8; 15 October 1993, 5; and 22 October 1993, 5.

30. See Ralph Della Cava, "Financing the Faith: The Case of Roman Catholicism," *Journal of Church and State* 35, no. 1 (1993): 37–59 for an argument that papal appointments have a pragmatic rationale and are not exclusively conservative.

31. Padre Andrés Girón, interview with author, Nueve Concepción, Guatemala, June 1992.

32. Dennis A. Smith, Presbyterian missionary and Coordinator, Per-

manent Assembly of Christian Groups, interview with author, Guatemala City, Guatemala, 16 January 1995.

33. Lernoux, *People of God*, 367; Crahan, "Religion and Democratization," 343–47; also see Michael Dodson and Laura Nuzzi O'Shaughnessy, *Nicaragua's Other Revolution: Religious Faith and Political Struggle* (Chapel Hill: University of North Carolina Press, 1990).

34. Lernoux, *People of God*, 379; Williams, *Catholic Church*, 68–88.

35. William M. LeoGrande, "Political Parties and Postrevolutionary Politics in Nicaragua," in *Political Parties and Democracy in Central America* ed. Louis W. Goodman, William M. LeoGrande, and Johanna Mendelson Forman (Boulder, Colo.: Westview, 1992), 192.

36. Michael Dodson, "Shifting Patterns of Religious Influence in Central America: The Case of Revolutionary Nicaragua" (paper presented at the meeting of the American Political Science Association, Chicago, Ill., September 1992), 21–22.

37. Lernoux, *People of God*, 379; Williams, *Catholic Church*, 70.

38. LeoGrande, "Political Parties," 197.

39. Phillip Wheaton, telephone interview with author, 20 September 1993; Crahan, "Political Parties," 345–47; also see Joseph E. Mulligan, S.J., *The Nicaraguan Church and the Revolution* (Kansas City, Mo.: Sheed and Ward, 1991).

40. Dodson, "Shifting Patterns," 26–28. Carol Ann Drogus concludes relative to the Catholic Church that "[h]ierarchies in some countries, notably Nicaragua and Brazil, are returning to a church-state model of power-brokering with the political elite reminiscent of the early part of this century," in "The Rise and Decline of Liberation Theology: Churches, Faith, and Political Change in Latin America," *Comparative Politics* (July 1995): 470.

41. *Latinamerica Press*, 21 August 1986, quoted in Lernoux, *People of God*, 405; Dodson and O'Shaughnessy, *Nicaragua's Other Revolution,* 191.

42. Author's interview with Wheaton; Paul Jeffrey, "Base Communities Struggling in Nicaragua," *Latinamerica Press*, 4 March 1993, 4.

43. Jorge Bardeguez, Antonio Valdivieso Ecumenical Center, interview with author, Managua, Nicaragua, 8 November 1993.

44. "Speculation Surrounds Church Bombings," *Latinamerica Press*, 12 October 1995, 2; "Who's Bombing Nicaragua's Churches?" *Latinamerica Press*, 7 September 1995, 1.

45. See Drogus, "Rise and Decline of Liberation Theology" and Jean Daudelin and W. E. Hewitt, who write that "[t]he size, the effective

mobilization capacity and the influence of the 'popular' Church appear not only to have been almost universally exaggerated but also to be everywhere declining." In Daudelin and Hewitt, "Latin American Politics: Exit the Catholic Church?" in *Organized Religion in the Political Transformation of Latin America*, ed. Satya R. Pattnayak (Lanham, Md.: University Press of America, 1995), 177.

46. *Latinamerica Press*, 5 November 1992, 3.

47. "Christian base communities after Santo Domingo—an interview with theologian Pablo Richard," *Latinamerica Press,* 3 June 1993, 5. In an interview with church historian Jorge Bardeguez in Managua, Nicaragua, he referred to the Santo Domingo documents as evidence that "the Church is going back to its most reactionary era," 8 November 1993.

48. "The problem is the church's unjust structure," *Latinamerica Press*, 5 November 1992, 7.

49. Lernoux, *People of God,* 153.

50. Daudelin and Hewitt, "Exit?", 188.

51. *Latinamerica Press*, 8 October 1992, 3.

52. "A Pivotal Conference Is Begun by Latin Bishops," *New York Times*, 13 October 1992.

53. Dodson and O'Shaughnessy, *Nicaragua's Other Revolution*, 84; also see, Pablo A. Deiros, "Protestant Fundamentalism in Latin America," in *Fundamentalisms Observed* ed. Martin E. Marty and R. Scott Appleby (Illinois: University of Chicago Press, 1991).

54. "Mas de 70 herides en zafarracho," *Prensa Libra* (Guatemala City), 20 August 1991, 14; and "Serrano: No hay guerra religiosa," *Siglo Vientiuno* (Guatemala City), 17 November 1992. A recent incident in Brazil indicates the underlying tension throughout Latin America. When a Protestant pastor destroyed a statue of Brazil's patron saint on the TV program *Awaken the Faith*, physical confrontations took place in the streets of Rio de Janeiro. More compromising Protestant leaders responded to widespread Catholic indignation. See "Religious Sparks in Brazil," *Latinamerica Press*, 26 October 1995, 1.

55. Dennis Wheeler, Director of PAVA and restaurant owner, interview with author, Antigua, Guatemala, 25 January 1993.

56. Mike Berg and Paul Pretiz, *The Gospel People* (Monrovia, Calif.: MARC, World Vision International/Latin America Mission, 1991), 111.

57. Eugene Daniels, *A Protestant Looks at the Catholic Church in Mission* (Monrovia, Calif.: Mission Advanced Research Center, World Vision International, 1993), 38–39.

58. For analyses of recent Catholic responses to the challenges of Protestantism in Latin America, see Edward L. Cleary and Hannah

Stewart-Gambino, eds., *Conflict and Competition: The Latin American Church in a Changing Environment* (Boulder, Colo.: Lynne Rienner, 1992).

59. Daniels, *Catholic Church in Mission*, 36.

60. John Hall, Professor of Mission, Nazarene Seminario, interview with author, San José, Costa Rica, 8 July 1993.

61. Annis, *God and Production*, 61–62, 80.

62. Berg and Pretiz, *Gospel People*, 110-11.

63. Roy Peterson, Director of External Relations, Summer Institute of Linguistics, interview with author, Guatemala City, Guatemala, 2 November 1993.

64. Author's interview with Wheaton.

65. Dale Whitman, Pastor and missionary to Guatemala, Christian Missionary Alliance, interview with author, DeLand, Florida, 15 November 1995.

66. CELA I was held in Buenos Aires in 1949, CELA II in Lima, Peru, in 1961, and CELA III in Buenos Aires in 1969.

67. Dodson and O'Shaughnessy, *Nicaragua's Other Revolution*, 58; and Kerry Ptacek, "U.S. Protestants and Liberation Theology," *Orbis*, (fall 1986): 433–41.

68. Dodson and O'Shaughnessy, *Nicaragua's Other Revolution*, 114.

69. "CEPAD: The Council of Evangelical Churches of Nicaragua," informational brochure, Managua, Nicaragua, 1993.

70. Author's interview with Bardeguez.

71. Tarrow, *Power in Movement*, 23.

72. Benjamín Cortés, Secretary General, Centro InterEclesia de Estudio Teológicos y Sociales (CIEETS), interview with author, Managua, Nicaragua, 11 November 1993.

73. Tarrow, *Power in Movement*, 24–25.

Chapter Five

Assessing the Political Impact of Protestantism in Central America

We were disappointed in [evangelical President of Guatemala] Serrano. There is a real solemness in the evangelical church now about the millions of quetzales [money in corruption scandals] disappearing and the rest. But the evangelicals are very resilient about it all, saying, 'Let's learn from this.'

> — Roy Peterson, Summer Institute
> of Linguistics, Guatemala, 1993

Guatemala is *not* a breeding ground for radical theology like Nicaragua is.

> — Dennis Smith, Presbyterian Church
> USA, Permanent Assembly of
> Christian Groups, Guatemala City,
> 1990

We have seen that Protestantism is a social movement in terms of presenting a challenge to Catholicism and secularism. What is the potential of this movement for challenging political and economic structures and the injustices they perpetuate in the society? If evangelical ideology and practice and community-building are gradually implanting a sense of empowerment among the poor, does that empowerment stop short of political influence? As the opening quote from Guatemala illustrates, having a president who happened to be an evangelical was an exercise in frustration and disillusionment. How can the Protestant movement exert an impact on the inequities of an economic system in which 2 percent of the population own 70 to 80 percent of the land? Thus far we have focused largely on microlevel aspects of religious change in Central America. Before we attempt to answer these macrolevel questions, let us briefly survey economic conditions in these countries.

Despite the geographical proximity and the close political and economic links between the United States and Central America, North Americans are unable to grasp the intensity and scope of poverty in Central America. The 1980s were a time of economic and social decline for that region as Cold War hostilities were debated in the United States but were waged in Central America. Massive amounts of U.S. aid went to El Salvador (about $5 billion), Honduras (about $2 billion), and Nicaragua (hundreds of millions to the contras and $674 million in postwar reconstruction). But the money was squandered in death, destruction, and corruption. The industrial and transportation infrastructures are now in worse shape than they were in the 1970s, the environment is severely damaged, illiteracy is greater, and the poverty rate is higher, running at about 70 percent throughout the region.[1]

For instance, Guatemala has approximately eleven million people, 46 percent of whom are under the age of fifteen years. A majority of the children are malnourished, and fewer than 60 percent of the population have access even to safe drinking water. In 1989 the U.N. Human Development Report classified 71 percent of the country's population as living in "absolute poverty."[2] The agrarian population, 55 percent of whom are indigenous, is being pushed to the capital city as title to their ancestral land is assumed by the government and by transnational agro-companies that grow crops for export. Urban poverty is reflected in spiraling crime rates. Some 85 street gangs operate, and vigilante groups are often the prevailing law.[3] The Guatemalan government only began inching toward democracy in 1985 with the election of President Cerezo, and it is still widely recognized that the military structure virtually controls the government. The country has been torn apart by a vicious civil war that is only winding down in the 1990s, after more than thirty years of fighting and an estimated 140,000 deaths. Guatemala still has the worst record for political killings and other human rights violations in Central America.[4]

Table 5.1 summarizes the discouraging statistics for the region and contrasts them to the opulence of the United States; only Costa Rica escapes the more depressing indicators. The reasons for the vast disparities that exist in the western hemisphere are complex

Table 5.1

Development Indicators for Selected Nations

	Population	% of Population Urban	Annual % Increase in Population	Literacy Rate % Male/Female	Life Expectancy Male/Female	GDP	HDI*
Costa Rica	3,300,000	49	2.2	93/93	74/79	$5,900	0.88
El Salvador	5,900,000	46	2.6	76/70	65/70	$2,500	0.58
Guatamala	10,600,000	38	3.1	63/47	62/67	$3,000	0.59
Honduras	5,500,000	46	2.8	76/71	66/71	$1,950	0.58
Nicaragua	4,400,000	62	2.7	57/57	62/68	$1,500	0.61
United States	263,200,000	75	0.7	97/97	72/79	$24,700	0.94

Human Development Index (HDI): This number was devised by the U.N. as a way to measure economic and human well-being. Raging from 0 to 1, it combines life expectancy, adult literacy, and purchasing power (the ability to buy necessities such as food, clothing, and shelter) into a sigle statistic. Even countries with low percapita GDP may rank high on the HDI - that is, if their people live relatively long, are mostly literate, and generate enough purchasing power to rise above poverty. Countries with high per capita GDP may still have low HDI rates, if income is highly concentrated in the upper classes, as it is in many Latin American nations. Note: HDI does not account for such factors as freedom, justice, and human rights.

Source: 1995 World Population Data Sheet and Human Development Report, 1995, The U.N. Development Program and have been thoroughly analyzed by political economists who concentrate on such words as colonialism, agro-export economies, bureaucratic-authoritarianism, dependency, and neoliberalism. Most recently, the governments of Central America are attempting to recover ground lost in the 1980s by following neoliberal directives from the International Monetary Fund and the World Bank. These directives entail such measures as "structural adjustments" that support a free market economy, free trade, privatization of services, deregulaton, and decentralization of the economy. Economic development in the neoliberal model seldom reaches the poor, certainly not in the short term.

These cold statistics and economic terms are lived by millions of unemployed adults, by countless numbers of homeless street children, by thousands of people who live their entire lives scavenging through garbage in the subculture of the dumps around growing cities, by millions of refugees uprooted by civil war, and by indigenous people in constant fear of sudden, arbitrary violence. These are the same people who are increasingly turning to the evangelical churches for solace and support and a sense of meaningfulness in life.

At the microlevel of neighborhood churches people are able to regain some control over their lives and counter feelings of hopelessness that result from intractable economic problems. We saw in chapter 4 that evangelical converts typically change their lifestyles after their "born-again experience," saving money while eschewing alcohol, smoking, amd spousal and child abuse. We saw that this religion appeals because it preaches for change at the individual and family level rather than for structural or political change. Feelings of political inefficacy are common among the poor, but conceivably anyone with the right inspiration can make changes in his or her personal life. We have argued that it is valid to analyze changes at a society's microlevel as well as at the usual macrolevel of economic and political policymaking. As Cecilia Loreto Mariz has written in a recent book about religion and poverty in Brazil,

> [a]lthough more limited in their consequences than larger political measures, the everyday attempts to improve living conditions by small groups of the poor and their families are equally important. The everyday struggles of the poor may not only solve an immediate need,

allowing a particular population to survive, but may also foster cultural transformations, producing a long-standing and less reversible change in the population.[5]

Numerous field studies have concluded that converts to evangelicalism discover new dignity in their emphasis on a personal relationship with Christ and become less fatalistic about their helplessness in the midst of socioeconomic upheavals. Gradually, perhaps over generations, many become more demanding of change in the political system because of subtle cultural transformations, even if they have adhered to a biblical framing that is apolitical.

One social movement aspect of personal life changes is that they are made in a community setting and will occur frequently enough to percolate up to the broader society. Note that this is almost the reverse process advocated by liberation theology, which *begins* with goals for the broader political-economic system, goals that have not resonated widely with the people. In contrast, the evangelical movement begins with personal acceptance and change in a community setting and then, conceivably, moves outward. In social movement terms, Protestantism has experienced successful recruitment, has mobilized through symbolic framing, has widened into the broader culture, has effected and formed alliances with some Catholics, has become somewhat institutionalized, and is starting to move into politics. Thus, at an evangelical conference held in Guatemala in 1994, participants explicitly asked the social movement question: "Since Guatemala is now 30 percent evangelical, why is the political, economic, and social situation still so bad?"

Let us examine the evidence that the Protestant movement in Central America is "contentious collective action" that challenges not only secular society, Catholicism, and traditional religion, but could also challenge the dominant political system. Social movements can play a crucial mediating role between communities and institutional politics.[6] This is beginning to occur, for instance, through formation of some religiously based political parties in Central America. However, it is less clear that the challenge of social movements in the region will escalate into what Sidney Tarrow calls a "cycle of protest." In this phase of social movement development the conflict heightens and spreads, forms alliances, has new unifying "master frames" for collective action, and has "sequences of intensified interaction between challengers and authorities which can end in reform, repression and sometimes revolution."[7] But genuine political opportunities must open up for this cycle of protest to occur, a precondition which is not present in much of Central America, certainly not in Guatemala. The mediating role of evangelicals in Guatemala is a minor political challenge thus far, and there Protestantism may remain a cultural movement that has its greatest impact at the local level and in gradual, long-term social change. This chapter examines the mediating role Protestants have played in recent electoral politics first in Guatemala, and then in the contrasting case of Nicaragua. As always, context is crucial for understanding movement dynamics, and three elements are particularly important for analysis of political opportunities available to the Protestant movement: original missionary patterns, leadership patterns, and the national political culture.

PROTESTANTS IN PRESIDENTIAL POLITICS IN GUATEMALA

In 1990 presidential candidate Jorge Serrano Elías surprised Guatemalans with his landslide win of 67 percent of the vote over newspaper publisher Jorge Carpio Nicolle (Carpio was assassinated in 1993). Serrano, head of the conservative party *Movimiento de Acción Solidaria* (MAS), was a dark horse—a businessman with sporadic ties to national politics and an evangelical. He was not the first Protestant president in Central America. General Efraín Ríos Montt achieved that distinction when he headed the coup d'etat of 1982. But Serrano was the first Protestant civilian to win an election in Central America. Serrano had served as head of the Council of State in the Ríos Montt government, an appointment gained from a family tie to Montt's church. In 1985 Serrano ran for President, had received only 13.8 percent of the vote.[8]

Serrano was a neo-Pentecostal member of the large urban church El Shaddai, having converted to Protestantism in 1977. He was a moderate in politics and in religion who was not as close to the messianic Ríos Montt as U.S. press accounts indicated. For instance, he had been banished from Guatemala for a time for criticizing the Lucas Garcia regime in the 1970s, and he had also criticized the secret tribunals of Ríos Montt's government. In the late 1980s Serrano was named to the Council on National Reconciliation (CNR) and earned praise for arranging face-to-face negotiations between the military and the guerrillas. His basic campaign platform in 1990 was simplistic and "Christian-oriented," stressing the importance of family unity, free enterprise economy but with social programs, obedience to law, and respect for human rights since "human dignity comes from God."[9] Serrano's form of evangelicalism was nonthreatening and inclusive— Catholics voted for him as well as fellow neo-Pentecostals.

For a time Serrano's most serious opponent was Rios Montt himself who had announced a bid for the presidency and was leading in the polls. However, the Guatemalan courts upheld a constitutional prohibition on the candidacy of any official who ever held office as the result of a coup, and so Rios Montt was disqualified. He responded by asking his followers to negate their ballots in a show of support for him, but most switched their support to Serrano instead—or stayed home.

Table 5.2

Correlation of Percent of Departmental Vote for Serrano
with Ranking of Departments by Percent of Indigenous Pop.,
Population, and Number of Protestant Churches per Capita
(N = 22 departments)

	Percent of Indigenous Pop. in Dept.	Population of Dept.	Number of Protestant Churches Per Capita
Percent Vote for Serrano			
Correlation (r)	.16	–.30	.23
Significance (two-tail test)	$p \leq .05$	$p \leq .05$	$p \leq .05$

What role did evangelicals play in electing this Latin American Protestant? Analysis of the election data underscores the importance of distinguishing the three categories of Protestants described in chapter 3: the traditional, historic Protestants; the Pentecostal majority; and the neo-Pentecostal upwardly mobile. Serrano and most of his evangelical supporters were from the neo-Pentecostal group not the majority of evangelicals who did not bother to vote at all. Table 5.2 presents correlations computed using aggregate data on the twenty-two departments of Guatemala provided by the Latin American Evangelical Center for Pastoral Studies (CELEP). The figures indicate a slight positive correlation between percent indigenous population and percent voting for Serrano, and a slightly stronger positive correlation between the density of Protestant churches and the vote for Serrano. The inverse correlation with population indicates that the more populated departments were less likely to give strong support to Serrano. Thus there is a statistically significant positive correlation, but a fairly weak one, between the more Protestant regions and the Protestant candidate's support.

Table 5.3 shows a breakdown of election returns by department as well as the number of Protestant churches per capita. Clearly Serrano's victory was fairly uniform across the country and was not concentrated in the most Protestant departments. The most significant fact about the election, however, is that less than half of those registered turned out to vote. These data together indicate that the Protestant constituency was *not* an important element in Serrano's victory. He could not rely on an evangelical voting bloc, but won instead by using television effectively and by campaigning among Catholics as well as Protestants against a relatively weak opponent. The Guatemalan tendency to withdraw from politics is still reinforced by the religious culture for the majority of evangelicals. Even when a respected evangelical was running for the presidency, Protestant pastors were not heavily involved in campaigning, and the believers did not go to the polls in large numbers.

Ríos Montt's strong showing in the public surveys prior to the election is an interesting aspect of this analysis. Ríos Montt is not a part of the more worldly evangelical circle that is seeking political reform. He is a demagogue and represented the apolitical Pentecostals even as he ran for political office. For instance, when asked about his political platform, Ríos Montt replied, "We don't need a written platform for it's already in the Bible . . . the Christian principles of good self-administration and character. . . . Our biggest problem is the disintegration of the family, but when you have a government of the family, this can make a gov-

Table 5.3
Percent Serrano Vote and
Number of Protestant Churches per Capita
for the 22 Departments of Guatemala

Department	Number of Protestant Churches Per Capita (1986)*	Percent of those Voting in 1991 who Voted for Serrano**
Guatemala	1,565	0.71
Baja Verapaz	1,356	0.66
El Quiché	1,289	0.69
Jalapa	1,073	0.46
Sacatepequez	1,018	0.62
Chiqimula	993	0.52
Huehuetenango	799	0.70
Alta Verapaz	774	0.59
Quetzaltenango	764	0.65
Sololá	749	0.68
Totonicapan	741	0.70
Jutiapa	709	0.59
San Marcos	706	0.69
Chimaltenango	669	0.74
Santa Rosa	625	0.68
Esquintla	587	0.73
Zacapa	566	0.74
Izabel	544	0.68
Suchitepequez	542	0.67
El Progreso	525	0.64
Average	808	0.68 (936,389 of 1,375,379 voting)

Source: General Director of Statistics, Servicio Evangelizador Para Améri-ca Latina (SEPAL). The SEPAL Survey, although the best data available, is only approximate. They counted 10,347 churches in 1986, but numerous small churches are unconnected to any organization and are not counted.
    ** from the Tribunal Supremo Elector

ernment of the nation." When asked about his policies to help the poor, he responded that "the poor must be born again," adding simply that he would ask the churches to provide help to the poor, since charity was one of their main jobs. Ríos Montt also said that "everyone who does not know the Word of God is an oppoient,"[10] which is an ominous statement from a man who presided over the destruction of over four hundred villages. In any case, Ríos Montt's detachment from government policies and institutions was evidently based on his religious beliefs. Ironically, the constituency he was appealing to had the same detachment and even disdain for the political system. They might express support for him as the evangelical who used to give sermons on the radio from the presidential palace and as the strongman who could restore order in a crime-ridden society, but they would not participate in electing him, or anyone else.

Thus two paradoxical trends among evangelicals were evident in the 1990 election. One trend was continuation of the traditional withdrawal from the sinful world of politics; the second, newer, trend is the politicization that is occurring, especially among the neo-Pentecostals, i.e., the more urban and upwardly mobile faction of evangelicals. The clearest example of the latter trend is Serrano himself. He ran a sophisticated low-budget campaign without alienating the evangelicals or the Catholics whose votes he desperately needed. In an interview Serrano described the contrast with his 1985 campaign when the Christian community severely criticized him for being in politics. In 1990, he noted, "evangelicals are more political every day."[11]

Edmundo Madrid is the former president of the Evangelical Alliance in Guatemala, a prominent umbrella organization of Pentecostal and neo-Pentecostal churches. He described the need for politicization at the height of Serrano's presidential campaign:

> We haven't had the influence on political leaders that we should. The early missionaries said we should not be involved in politics. Somehow we believed this, but now we see that it's a mistake to leave public things to corrupt people. We are trying to teach our people that they should not be afraid. . . . The one good thing we learned from liberation theology is the importance, the need, to be involved in politics.[12]

This viewpoint of Madrid and other evangelical leaders is partly influenced by self-interest, given that their organizations remain a minority in Guatemala, and evangelicals are sometimes harrassed by government authorities. For example, Madrid feared that "Carpio as president would be anti-evangelical because he is old Catholic." Madrid was more candid than candidate Serrano regarding the intense rivalry that exists between the evangelicals and what he characterized as "the idol-worshipping Catholics."[13]

A study paper that was circulated among Protestant organizations in 1987 entitled *The Political Task of Evangelicals: Ideas for a New Guatemala* outlines reasons for politicization that go beyond self-interest. The paper was produced by an ad hoc group called the Christian Committee of Reflection, another organization that exemplifies the increasing institutionalization of Protestantism. The document calls for believers to become active in social and political work as well as evangelism. Thus it provides evidence that some Protestants are becoming more aware of their potential to act as a force for social change as they move from the periphery to the center of Guatemalan society.

What is remarkable about *The Political Task of Evangelicals* is that it recognizes government responsibility for social and economic problems in Guatemala and Christian responsibility for being involved at the local and national level in effecting change. This approach is far different from the traditional Pentecostal emphasis on the Second Coming as the miraculous source of peace and justice in society. It does not limit believers to a focus on salvation and self-discipline, but asks them to move outward into the political world. What is also remarkable about the document is its naive faith that timid social programs and democratic elections alone will be enough to counter the extreme hardships and inequities that exist in Guatemala. The report encourages development programs for the poor, but remains preoccupied with moderate reforms and anticommunism.

As political events unfolded in the early 1990s in Guatemala, the trust that Edmundo Madrid and many other neo-Pentecostals placed in Serrano was abused. In May 1993 Serrano attempted a coup by ordering the dissolution of the congress, and the supreme court and a partial suspension of the Constitution. He then declared that he would rule by decree indefinitely. The coup attempt followed weeks of futile efforts to implement controversial neoliberal policies such as raising electricity rates, privatizing energy production and other state enterprises, and cutting meager social services. It is likely that military hard-liners urged Serrano to be the civilian frontman for an old-fashioned military coup in order to break the governmental deadlock. However, in a courageous and surprising turn of events, popular demonstrations and international outrage at Serrano's power grab resulted in a "counter-coup" by more moderate military leaders. Serrano was forced to step down. Within two weeks, the Guatemalan Congress selected Human Rights Procurator Ramiro de León Carpio to serve out the remainder of Serrano's term as president.[14] President Serrano, the great hope of Guatemalan neo-Pentecostals, eventually was found to have embezzled government funds and was forced to leave the country. One former colleague of Serrano estimates that the former president was worth over $14 million when he fled Guatemala. He is now living in comfortable exile in Panama under the protection of the government there and extradition is unlikely.[15]

Ramiro de León Carpio finished out the presidential term as an ineffectual, but at least uncorrupted, head of state.[16] In Guatemala's third presidential general election on January 7, 1996, only 36.88 percent of the registered electorate participated in selecting the former mayor of Guatemala City, Alvaro Arzú, as the new president. Arzú is a conservative businessman of the National Advanced Party (PAN), and he faced Alfonso Portillo of the Republican Guatemalan Front (FRG) in this run-off election.[17] The low turnout was a disappointment to many. The government had campaigned for a good showing, as well as guerrilla leaders, and Guatemala's Catholic bishops, who wrote a pastoral letter that advocated voting "as a way of changing a democracy that has been more formal than real."[18]

PROSPECTS FOR THE DEVELOPMENT
OF DEMOCRACY IN GUATEMALA

What can be said about democracy in Guatemala in the wake of the 1990 presidential election, the thwarted coup d'etat, and the 1996 election? The most obvious point is that Guatemala's democracy is extremely fragile. As the bishop's letter noted, it is only in terms of a narrow structural definition, that "democracy" is operating in Guatemala. The low voter turnout for all elections dampens any sanguine view that long-lasting democracy has arrived in Guatemala. Over 80 percent of indigenous women, for instance, have not even bothered to register to vote.[19] As one researcher in Guatemala City put it, "The high abstention rate is itself a significant political statement. People aren't convinced that the electoral system is adequate to address the fundamental problems of Guatemala."[20]

A few positive signs for reformist government are emerging in the midst of the chaos and inequities, however. During the 1990 and 1995 elections the Supreme Electoral Tribunal (TSE) sustained the Guatemalan constitution and declared General Efraín Ríos Montt ineligible to run for president because he had been the participant in a coup d'etat. The TSE was under enormous pressure to find a way to rule in favor of a Ríos Montt candidacy because of his popularity and because he had been elected as president of the congress. The TSE held firm, however, and in August 1995 the Supreme Court ordered Ríos Montt to step down as congressional president to face charges of usurpation of power.[21] The outcry of public opinion in Guatemala City after Serrano attempted an auto-coup and the dramatic choice of the Human Rights Ombudsman as the new president were also signs of democratic awareness. Furthermore, prodded by international pressure, one of the first steps taken by President Arzú was to discharge many colonels and eight of the sixteen generals in Guatemala's armed forces, as well as hundreds of corrupt police officials.[22] It is far too early to assess the sincerity of this crackdown, but if Arzú is able to exert authentic civilian rule over the military, rather than the usual facade, perhaps a reformist democracy will become a possibility. Meanwhile, for evangelicals, Ríos Montt's disgrace, in addition to Serrano's, compounds their disillusionment with national politics.

Political scientist Peter Smith has identified five major limitations constraining democratic development in Latin America, and all of them apply to Guatemala. First is the continuing presence of the military, which severely limits the policy options of the civilian officeholders. Second is the virtual absence of the Left as voters are simply asked to choose between moderate Right and extreme Right candidates. This leads to the third point that open debate about major economic reform does not occur; moderate and rightist public officials will not seriously consider land reform or overhaul of the wage structure. Fourth is the presence of widespread human rights abuses, which tragically persist in Guatemala. Finally, Smith notes the common practice of unilateral, undemocratic decision-making in regard to economic policy as a constraint.[23] The significance of recognizing these limitations on government is that scholars have traditionally placed too much emphasis on electoral processes rather than these governing processes in defining democracy. Given this long-standing emphasis, it is not surprising that the authors of *The Political Task of Evangelicals* were overly optimistic about achieving socioeconomic improvements simply through democratic elections. Nevertheless, this neo-Pentecostal branch of the evangelicals will probably continue engaging in presidential elections. They were not particularly organized or effective in Serrano's campaign, and were they divided and distracted by Ríos Montt in 1995. But Serrano's victory did inspire many neo-Pentecostals to become involved in politics despite his subsequent downfall. A few of the larger Protestant churches in Guatemala City have even been conducting political rallies and workshops, aware that, above all, they must select strong and trustworthy candidates.

After thirty years of military rule Guatemala only turned to electoral politics in 1985, and as we have seen, the results for the people thus far have not been encouraging. This brings us full circle to the reasons many Guatemalans are joining Protestant churches. People who are discouraged by a political system that does not deliver on its promises find hope instead in stronger families, in neighborhood churches, and in religious experiences.

As discussed previously, being members of an evangelical church means being active in the community, not being isolated. When we look closely at villages and neighborhoods, we see more evidence of democratic values in Guatemala than we would suspect from the half-hearted national elections. Locally-based human rights organizations such as the Mutual Support Group (GAM), an urban organization of nearly 12,000 women who have lost family members to political violence, and its rural counterpart, the Confederation of Guatemalan Widows (CONAVIGUA), have challenged the government for years demanding information and justice. In 1996 these two organizations joined with other human rights groups, including Protestant churches, to form a political party called the New Guatemalan Democratic

Front (FDNG). The four month old FDNG surprised everyone by winning six of eighty seats in Congress in the November elections. These six activists, including three indigenous females, now find themselves part of the government they have long opposed.[24]

In addition to supporting human rights, the churches have become a major resource compensating for state incapacity in Guatemala. The governmental response to massive poverty in Guatemala in recent decades has been quite simple—encourage nongovernmental charitable organizations to take on the job. Thus Guatemalan political leaders have tapped into the pervasive network of religious resources wherever they can because the financial base of the government is simply inadequate to provide aid to poor communities. The plurality of such charitable organizations in recent decades has been Protestant religious bodies. For instance, as was noted in chapter 1, the government's National Reconstruction Committee maintains contracts for development projects with nongovernmental organizations (NGO's) in an attempt to coordinate various charitable projects. Of 150 such projects that were on file in this office in 1992, 135 were with Protestant organizations. These contractual projects often have foreign mission funding, but, importantly, they are usually administered by resident volunteers at the village and neighborhood level. For instance, Protestant organizations sponsor the building of schools, clinics, tree nurseries, potable water systems, and the development of microbusinesses. Such projects, of course, are in addition to the supporting work of thousands of individual congregations ministering to their members.

There are other signs of a local populism emerging in towns with large Pentecostal contingents. For instance, 8 percent of national tax funds in Guatemala are supposed to be distributed for local development, but this money often disappears. Now there are reports of Pentecostal groups demanding of the local mayor that the tax money be used righteously.[25] Pentecostals in Guatemala generally tend to withdraw from national politics because it is sinful and "of this world" to be involved in party politics. But it is a coherent ideology for them to be motivated to participate in local politics out of a righteous ferver, a rejection of the corruption of the world in their very midst.

Figure 5.1 presents one of the findings from the first national study of political culture ever undertaken in Guatemala. In their extensive 1993 survey of a random sample of twelve hundred Guatemalans the researchers assessed Protestantism as a variable influencing community participation and drew the following conclusion

> various 'non-Catholic' Christian groups, largely Protestant fundamentalists, exhibit significantly (<.001) higher communal participation than do Catholics. We also found that those with no religion had the lowest level of participation. . . . Apparently, these new groups do help stimulate local level participation.[26]

To underscore the evidence that religion matters for participation, the researchers also report that communal participation was not at all related to education, ethnicity, gender, age or urban/rural distinctions, but was significantly associated with religiosity.[27]

What conclusions can we draw about the link between Protestantism and democracy in Guatemala? Some neo-Pentecostals will continue to try to influence national politics from their self-interest in protecting religious freedom and trying to improve the economy, and from a sense of righteousness about fixing the system. However, their impact on the political system will be negligible

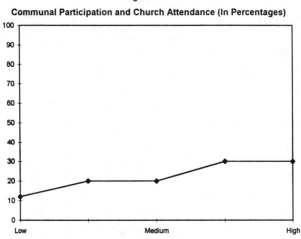

Figure 5.1

Communal Participation and Church Attendance (In Percentages)

Source: "Guatemalan Values and the Prospects for Democratic Development"
Mitchell A. Seligson & Joel M. Jutkowitz, University of Pittsburgh, 1994.

in the foreseeable future because of their political inexperience and because authentic political opportunities do not yet exist in Guatemala, given the persistent military dominance. At the local grassroots level prospects for increasing democratic participation are somewhat brighter, and Protestantism is making a contribution. The Guatemalan Democracy Study provides empirical evidence regarding the hypothesis that becoming an evangelical has an empowering effect for some people—evangelicals participate more than Catholics or nonreligious. But Guatemalans do not have a democratic heritage, and, of all Central Americans, they are the least likely to express an attitude supporting a democratic political order.[28] Rather than pursuing an abstract concept of "democracy," a priority for Guatemalans is simply to find a sense of security. Thus the possibility of Protestantism as a social movement escalating to a cycle of protest in Guatemala is remote indeed.[29] Instead, the evangelical churches are attempting to meet the needs of the people and fostering democratic attitudes at a much more modest level.

PROGRESSIVE PENTECOSTALS
IN NICARAGUA

We now turn to an examination of Protestants and politics in the contrasting case of Nicaragua—the only country in the region to experience a full-scale revolution in this century. We begin with a look at original Protestant missionary patterns in Nicaragua, which are also distinctive for the region. Table 2.1 in chapter 2 listed the largest U.S. evangelical organizations in the five nations and revealed the variation in Protestant missions among these neighboring countries. This variation goes back at least to the "comity" agreements and has been reinforced by more recent political developments. For instance, note from the listing that only in Nicaragua do the largest U.S. evangelical groups include the more progressive and ecumenical denominations, such as the Mennonite Central Committee, the Presbyterian Church USA, the United Methodist Church, and American Baptist Churches USA. The prominence of these historic churches creates a fascinating and unique dynamic in Nicaragua. These particular churches actively lobbied against the Nicaraguan contras in Washington in the 1980s,

and they sent financial aid as well as missionaries in support of
the Sandinistas.[30] For example, the organization Witness for Peace,
which recruits members from these same churches in the U.S.,
sent three teams a month to Nicaragua to testify against the contras and maintained a waiting list of hundreds throughout the
1980s. These U.S. missionaries still work closely with Nicaraguan
Protestant leaders, and a majority still support the overall goals
of the leftists, as opposed to the neoliberal agenda of the Violeta
Chamorro administration.[31]

It is a grave disservice to most evangelicals in Nicaragua to
assume that they were ever pawns of U.S. government policy because their Protestant roots are in the U.S. Yet this assumption
was made by social scientists and by the Sandinista leaders themselves in the first years after the 1979 victory. Despite the fact
that a large evangelical sector supported the FSLN, many Protestant churches were arbitrarily seized between 1982 and 1983, and
a propaganda campaign against preachers and believers was implemented by the Sandinista Defense Committee.[32] These seizures
were in addition to the Sandinistas' infamous forced relocation of
the indigenous Miskito population on Nicaragua's eastern coast.
The Miskitos were also largely Protestant, having been converted
by Moravian missionaries in the 1840s.[33]

Eventually the FSLN recovered from its mistakes and recon-
ciled with most of the evangelical population, as summarized by
Roberto Zub Kurylowicz, a professor of theology in Managua:

> A historical fact is that no president of Nicaragua before Daniel Or-
> tega, nor any government has ever had such a close relationship with
> the Protestants as the Sandinista Government. President Ortega and
> other commanders of the Revolution attended various worship ser-
> vices, conferences, and evangelical revivals. . . . Dr. Gustavo A. Para-
> jon, Pastor of the First Baptist Church of Managua, was chosen by
> President Ortega as a "Notable Citizen". . . . In the period of the
> Sandinista Government, there have been more Bibles distributed and
> sold than under any other government.[34]

The Sandinistas' overtures to the Protestants were eventually
prompted by the support that many church leaders had actively
demonstrated for the revolution. On the other hand, many in the
Catholic hierarchy were retreating from Sandinismo at the time.
As one scholar in Managua succinctly explained to me, "When

the Catholic bourgeoisie here reacted against the revolution—reinforced by the Vatican—the revolution searched for a replacement church."[35] Although more attention has been given to the dramatic political struggles of the Catholic Church in Nicaragua,[36] many Protestants have been heavily involved in the politics of the revolution, often in support of the Sandinistas.

A nation's missionary experience is an important starting point for understanding the political impact of Protestants. Perhaps the most important contribution of missionaries in Nicaragua has been to encourage and support leadership development within Nicaragua itself, which we will now examine. We noted in chapter 3 that one way Pentecostalism empowers the poor is by making the churches are accessible to lay leadership. Virtually anyone with the "gift of the Spirit" can seize the opportunity to be leader in a church and often, the community. This is undoubtedly also true and important in Nicaragua.[37] However, an impressive array of religious leadership *institutions* have also emerged in Nicaragua, encouraged by missionaries, but clearly national. This is again related to the strong presence of the historic denominations in the country. These Presbyterians, Methodists, American Baptists, etc. have more of a written theology and institutional heritage than Pentecostals, and it was a natural step for these Protestants to form organizations early on.

For instance, we have already met the *Centro InterEclesial de Estudios Teológicos y Sociales* (CIEETS) in Managua, a seminary that was founded in 1985 by eighty-five Nicaraguan evangelical churches. In addition to CIEETS is the *Seminario Bautista* and the Antonio Valdivieso Ecumenical Center (CAV). The CAV was founded by a Catholic priest and a Baptist minister in 1979 "to help Catholics and Protestants reflect on this new experience of the revolution."[38] Now it operates two divisions: one for *reflexión*, i.e., "reflection" through leadership training, workshops, symposiums, and research, and another for social action and development projects. Another prestigious religious organization in Nicaragua we have met already is the *Comité Evangélico Pro Ayuda al Desarrollo* (CEPAD), which was formed after the 1972 earthquake. Another group is The Foundation for Victims of the War, founded by Methodists in 1987 and now led by Sonia Guiterrez. The leaders of these organizations often work together, and in interviews they volunteer high praise for each other, indicating a close-knit community. For instance, Sonia Guiterrez is also president of CAV; and the secretary general of CIEETS was the first executive director of CEPAD.

Separation of church and state is an alien concept in Nicaragua, despite guaranteed separation of church and state in the Nicaraguan constitution. Religious leaders are also highly visible public opinion leaders, at least in Managua where they regularly make the press opinion pages. They are sometimes outspoken in their criticisms of the current neoliberal policies, as illustrated by these representative comments:

> I'm a socialist at heart, like a lot of evangelicals here. I really don't think that within the strictures of a global market, Nicaragua can ever stand on its feet. If you have a government from the bourgeoisie sector, they defend the lifestyle of that sector.[39]
>
> Chamorro is sincere when she says she doesn't discriminate. It's more a result of the fact that she's wealthy and she believes the problems will be solved by the wealthy and technocrats. It's not a conscious discrimination, but a result of class.[40]
>
> Production is very, very low. We export $250 million a year and import over $800 million! We are a country without the capability to produce our own food. In the beginning, I expected a better government from Chamorro; they talked in a good way about agricultural reform. But they have not followed through.[41]

Both CEPAD and CAV leaders have entered into very public confrontations with the government. For instance, a few years ago the minister of finance issued a tax decree on Protestant, but not Catholic, organizations, with an especially stiff tax on CEPAD. It was clearly a case of harrassment, and eventually the supreme court issued a writ causing the tax decree to be revoked. The extent to which religion and politics overlap in Nicaragua is revealed in a complaint made by the head of the Baptist Convention of Nicaragua: "We don't see any reason why we should live as second-class citizens while the government treats Catholics as first-class citizens."[42]

Given these tensions, it is a tribute to CEPAD's leadership that occasionally the government must still turn to the organization for assistance, as during the aftermath of the 1992 tidal wave. The government was unprepared to help disaster victims, but CEPAD had warehouses of rice as well as local pastors and committees in place to give out supplies in the fishing towns one day after the disaster.[43] CEPAD has also served as an intermediary between the government and various rebel groups, both during the Sandinista regime and more recently. They tried to negotiate peace with the Miskito population and the Sandinistas in the mid-1980s and still have dozens of peace commissions around the country in places where the *contras* are rearming (the *recontras*).[44] As is the case throughout Central America, Protestant organizations have been an invaluable resource for the government, given the reality of state incapacity in these countries.

These prominent leadership groups in Nicaragua are generally identified with the ecumenical branch of the Protestant movement, which is linked to the World Council of Churches, the mainline U.S. churches active in Nicaragua, and the liberation theologians within the Catholic Church. They are part of the Latin American Council of Churches (CLAI), an ecumenical organization founded in 1982 to bring together these activists from many Latin American nations. The ecumenical churches in Latin America have often been at odds with the much larger Pentecostal branch of Protestantism over theological and political concerns. However, in Nicaragua, as we have seen, the ecumenical churches are particularly well established. They are not expanding, however, and are more than willing to work with the thriving Pentecostals. The Pentecostals are also well established, have large numbers of followers, and are beginning to seek leadership training. The usual tension between Pentecostal and ecumenical churches has been replaced by an atmosphere of mutual respect. As Professor Jorge Pixley explained,

There is broad evangelical cooperation in Nicaragua, more than in any other Central American nation, and Nicaraguan Baptists are at the center of that. The earthquake of 1972 was a catalyst for union through CEPAD. . . . Protestant churches in Nicaragua have had the space to develop autonomously.[45]

One tense incident between the ecumenical and Pentecostal branches of Protestantism in Nicaragua ironically demonstrates the norm of cooperation. In the 1980s the Assemblies of God Church withdrew from CEPAD and attempted to form its own interdenominational organization in Nicaragua. The Assemblies of God, as the largest member church, apparently wanted more power than they had within CEPAD.[46] It is also probable that the Assemblies of God wanted the disassociation because CEPAD was too political for their liking. The split could have been devastating for CEPAD, but only a handful of churches chose to go with the Assemblies of God evangelicals, leaving CEPAD as an umbrella organization for over sixty denominations, largely Pentecostal. Under the skillful leadership of Gustavo Parajon CEPAD unites extraordinarily diverse religious groups to assist the poor.

The Protestant church in Nicaragua has flourished during the last twenty years, just as it has elsewhere in Central America. Respondents in interviews consistently numbered evangelicals in the country at approximately five hundred thousand or roughly 20 percent of the population. We have discussed Protestant leadership organizations in Nicaragua, but what about the church members? Are evangelicals a potentially unified political bloc? If so, are they likely to be political leftists, like many of the intellectual leaders, or are they more likely to be withdrawn from politics according to the common image of Pentecostals? How does the political culture in Nicaragua influence evangelical attitudes toward participation? Fortunately, some suggestive survey data are available to address these questions—at least for Protestants in Managua. In late 1991 Roberto Zub of CIEETS conducted a survey of Protestants in Nicaragua: forty-three questions were asked of 248 adults from twenty-four representative evangelical churches in Managua, mostly dealing with the 1990 elections and political attitudes.[47] Zub's sample included two denominations which are strongly Pentecostal in their theology (the Assembly of God and the Four Square Church), plus the more ecumenical Baptist denomination and three others that fall somewhere in between.

Zub found that an extraordinary 90 percent of the Protestants said they voted in the 1990 elections, with little variation among the different denominations. The respondents were also consistent in reporting that their churches did not campaign for a particular party in any way (98.4 percent). The vote itself (Table 5.4) was fairly polarized among the evangelicals: almost 65 percent of the two Pentecostal denominations voted for Chamorro's UNO party, whereas about 39 percent of the Baptists voted for the administration. In addition, the survey indicates that across the board, these Protestants were far more willing than the general population to experiment among other parties. Only about 3 percent of the national vote went to all the other parties, but in this sample 10.4 percent voted for parties other than the two major ones.

Table 5.4
Party Voted for in 1990 Nicaraguan National Election,
by Denominational Sample (%)

Party	Assembly of God	4-Square Church	Christian Mission	Church of Christ	Church of God	Baptist
UNO	60.7	68.8	58.5	45.2	38.5	38.8
FSLN	19.6	15.6	31.7	41.9	23.1	40.8
Liberal	1.8	0.0	0.0	3.2	7.7	10.2
Others	7.2	9.4	7.3	3.2	18.0	6.0
No Vote	10.7	6.3	2.4	6.5	12.8	4.0

Source: Compiled from survey of 248 adults taken in 1991, Roberto Zub Kury-lowicz, *Protestantismo y elecciones en Nicaragua* (Managua, Nicaragua: Ediciones Nicarao, 1993), p. 66.

There are clear signs from other questions in the survey that the Pentecostal vote was less *for* UNO than *against* the Sandinistas (FSLN). For instance, Zub found that only 10.5 percent of his total sample were leaning toward the UNO party before the election; 29 percent were favoring the FSLN (mostly among the ecumenical churches); and 35.9 percent had no preferences at all. He also found that 64.2 percent of the two older Pentecostal churches regarded their relationship with the FSLN as "bad," probably remembering the early days of aggression against their churches by some Sandinistas. In contrast, 47 percent of the Baptists and 61.3 percent of the Church of Christ members found relations with the Sandinistas to be "good" or "excellent."[48] As a final indicator that the vote was not a ringing endorsement of UNO, Zub found that the majority (56.9 percent) of his sample wanted unspecified "major change" for Nicaragua. That strong a desire for major change is a primary factor in the defeat of the sitting government in 1990, the FSLN. More than coincidentally, the 56.9 percent in favor of strong change is a figure very close to that which UNO obtained nationwide in the elections (54.7 percent).

Thus, other than considerable Baptist and Church of Christ loyalty to the Sandinistas, most of these Protestants are not closely linked to any political party. When Zub asked if an evangelical can be affiliated with a political party, almost 51 percent said yes, the majority of that 51 percent being Baptist and Church of Christ members. But 48 percent said no to party *affiliation*. However, Zub went one step further to obtain his most interesting finding by asking, "Should an Evangelical Party be organized in Nicaragua?" This question produced a great deal of consensus among the Protestants, with almost 71 percent answering yes. Thus the 51 percent who okayed affiliation with a party, rose to 71 percent with the idea of forming and directing their own party.[49] Zub noted that this question brought the most effusive responses, such as "hallelujah" and "if there is an evangelical government, Christ will reign through it, and they will make a better distribution of wealth and justice."[50]

As a verification of Zub's finding, in February 1992 the Party of National Justice (PJN) was formed in Nicaragua as an evangelical party whose current leader is an International Baptist. In November 1992 the *Movimiento Evangélico Popular* (MEP) was formed by Rev. Miguel Angel Casco as a decidedly leftist political party seeking political and economic transformation for a more just society.[51] In August 1995 another explicitly Christian political party was formed in time to prepare for the October 1996 national elections. This party is called "Fuerza Cristiana" (Christian Force) and is comprised of both Catholic and evangelical churches with the vague goal of "seeking the moralization of politics, the democratization of society, and property ownership." Its founders also stated their strong dissatisfaction with Antonio Lacayo, the conservative heir apparent to Violetta Chamorro.[52] In a crowded field of thirty-two political parties these fledgling groups have an uphill battle against the present front-runner in presidential politics in the country, the right-wing former mayor of Managua, Arnoldo Aleman.[53] What is significant for our analysis is that these unapologetic Christians are hardly apolitical, "otherworldly" Pentecostals. In Nicaragua these evangelicals from the poorest segments of society are clamoring for political power.

In the chapter 6, we will draw some conclusions from the disparate experiences of Guatemala and Nicaragua in mixing evangelicalism and politics. We will also review our general analysis of Protestantism in Central America as a social movement in process.

NOTES

1. Douglas Farah, "The Lost Decade: Central America Is Staggering under Its '80s Legacy," *The Washington Post National Weekly Edition*, 14–20 June 1993, 6.

2. U.N. Development Programme, *Human Development Report 1993* (New York: 1993), 159 and 171.

3. "Urban Violence Rocks City," *Latinamerica Press*, 21 September 1995, 4.

4. On October 8, 1995, the army massacred eleven campesinos who had recently returned to Guatemala from exile in Mexico. The soldiers opened fire after a group of indigenous people criticized the military. Regarding human rights statistics, the Amnesty International statement of principles reads: "Amnesty International is often asked to compare the human rights records of different countries. It does not and cannot do this. . . . Statistical or other generalized comparisons can never measure the impact of human rights abuses on the victims, their families, and societies of which they are part." See Amnesty International U.S.A., *Guatemala: The Human Rights Record* (U.K.: Amnesty International Publications, 1987); *Honduras: Human Rights Violations* (U.K.: Amnesty International Publications, 1988); *Nicaragua: The Human Rights Record, 1986–1989* (U.K.: Amnesty International Publications, 1989). For further human rights research, see Thomas B. Jabine and Richard P. Claude, eds., *Human Rights and Statistics* (Philadelphia: University of Pennsylvania Press, 1992). Also see Ricardo Falla, *Massacres in the Jungle: Ixcan, Guatemala, 1975–1982* (Boulder, Colo.: Westview, 1994).

5. Cecilia Loreto Mariz, *Coping with Poverty: Pentecostals and Christian Base Communities in Brazil* (Philadelphia: Temple University Press, 1994), 4.

6. Sonia E. Alvarez and Arturo Escobar, "Conclusion: Theoretical and Political Horizons of Change in Contemporary Latin American Social Movements," in *The Making of Social Movements in Latin America: Identity, Strategy, and Democracy* (Boulder, Colo.: Westview, 1992), 326.

7. Sidney Tarrow, *Power in Movement: Social Movements, Collective Action and Politics* (New York: Cambridge University Press, 1994), 154.

8. Jorge Serrano Elías, interview with author, Guatemala City, Guatemala, 9 July 1990.

9. Author's interview with Serrano.

10. General Efraín Ríos Montt, interview with author, Guatemala City, Guatemala, 11 July 1990.

11. Author's interview with Serrano.

12. Edmundo Morales Madrid, 1990 President of *Alianza Evangélica de Guatemala*, interview with author, Guatemala City, Guatemala, 9 July 1990.

13. Author's interview with Madrid.

14. David Loeb, "Self-Coup/Counter-Coup: Serrano Is Out; What Comes Next?" *Report on Guatemala,* 14 (summer 1993): 2.

15. "Serrano on the Lam," *Latinamerica Press*, 4 April 1996.

16. For a glowing journalistic account of Ramiro de León Carpio's presidency see Alvaro Vargas Llosa and Santiago Aroca, *Riding the Tiger: Ramiro de León Carpio's Battle for Human Rights in Guatemala* (Miami: Brickell Communications, 1995).

17. "Arzú Takes Over in Guatemala," *Latinamerica Press*, 18 January 1996.

18. "Left Fights Electoral Indifference," *Latinamerica Press*, 17 August 1995, 3.

19. "Left Fights Indifference."

20. Dennis Smith, Latin American Evangelical Center for Pastoral Studies, interview with author, Guatemala City, Guatemala 12 January 1991.

21. "Voter Turnout Low in Guatemala," *The Huntsville Times*, 13 November 1995, A3.

22. Julia Preston, "Guatemalan Shakes Up Army and the Police," *New York Times*, 7 February 1996.

23. Peter H. Smith, "Crisis and Democracy in Latin America," *World Politics* 43 (July 1991): 608-34.

24. "In Guatemala's Male-Ruled Politics, Activist Widows Break into Congress," *Christian Science Monitor*, 16 January 1996, 7. The names of the three new activist, indigenous congresswomen are Nineth Montenegro, Roslina Tuyuc, and Manuela Alvarado.

25. Dennis Smith, Latin American Evangelical Center for Pastoral Studies, interview with author, Guatemala City, Guatemala, 16 January 1995.

26. Mitchell A. Seligson and Joel M. Jutkowitz, *Guatemalan Values and the Prospects for Democratic Development* (Development Associates/University of Pittsburgh/Asociación de Investigación y Estudios Sociales (ASIES), 1994), 91.

27. Seligson and Jutkowitz, *Guatemalan Values*, 90.

28. Seligson and Jutkowitz, *Guatemalan Values*, 119.

29. Also see David Stoll's even more pessimistic assessment in "'Jesus is Lord of Guatemala': Evangelical Reform in a Death-Squad State," in *Accounting for Fundamentalisms: The Dynamic Character of Movements*, ed. Martin E. Marty and R. Scott Appleby (Illinois: University of Chicago Press, 1994), 99–123.

30. Allen D. Hertzke, *Representing God in Washington: The Role of Religious Lobbies in the American Polity* (Knoxville: University of Tennessee Press, 1988), 129–34.

31. Gary Campbell, director of the Antonio Valdivieso Ecumenical Center (CAV), interview with author, Managua, Nicaragua, 9 November 1993.

32. Roberto Zub Kurylowicz, *Protestantismo y Elecciones en Nicaragua* (Managua, Nicaragua: Centro InterEclesial de Estudios Teológicos y Sociales, 1993), 69.

33. Roger S. Greenway, "Protestant Missionary Activity in Latin America," in *Coming of Age: Protestantism in Contemporary Latin America*, ed. Daniel R. Miller, (Lanham, Md.: University Press of America), 180; author's interview with Jorge Pixley, Professor of Bible at Seminario Bautista, Managua, Nicaragua, 10 November 1993.

34. Zub, *Protestantismo*, 70.

35. Jorge Bardeguez, Research Associate at the Antonio Valdivieso Ecumenical Center (CAV), interview with author, Managua, Nicaragua, 9 November 1993.

36. For example, Dodson and O'Shaughnessy, *Nicaragua's Other Revolution*; John M. Kirk, *Politics and the Catholic Church in Nicaragua* (Gainesville: University Press of Florida, 1992); Penny Lernoux, *People of God: The Struggle for World Catholicism* (New York: Viking, 1986); Edward A. Lynch, *Religion and Politics in Latin America: Liberation Theology and Christian Democracy* (New York: Praeger, 1991); And Philip J. Williams, *The Catholic Church and Politics in Nicaragua and Costa Rica* (Pittsburgh: University of Pittsburgh Press, 1989).

37. What we have noted elsewhere regarding leadership opportunities in Pentecostalism is also true for other Protestants: "the Moravian parson was the unelected mayor of most Miskito (Nicaragua) villages," Bruce Nichols, "Religious Conciliation between the Sandinistas and the East Coast Indians of Nicaragua," in *Religion, The Missing Dimension of Statecraft*, ed. Douglas Johnston and Cynthia Sampson, (New York: Oxford University Press, 1994), 67.

38. Author's interview with Campbell.

39. Author's interview with Pixley.

40. Author's interview with Parajon.

41. Author's interview with Cortes.

42. Author's interviews with Parajon and Pixley; and "Nicaraguan Government Goes after Evangelicals," *Latinamerica Press*, 10 September 1992, 3.

43. Author's interview with Pixley.

44. Author's interview with Parajon; also see Nichols, "Religious Conciliation," regarding CEPAD's peace negotiations on the East Coast.

45. Author's interview with Pixley.

46. Author's interviews with Cortes, Pixley, Bardeguez.

47. Zub, *Protestantismo.*

48. Zub, *Protestantismo,* 68.

49. Zub, *Protestantismo,* 74.

50. Zub, *Protestantismo,* 101.

51. Reverend Miguel Angel Casco, president of *Concilio Evangélico de Promoción and Renovación Social* and founder of *Movimiento Evangelico Popular (MEP)*, interview with author, Managua, Nicaragua, 12 November 1993. Interviews with Pixley, Campbell, and Bardeguez all confirm the information about the progressive goals of the MEP.

52. "New Political 'Christian Force' Is Formed," *La Prensa*, 8 September 1995, 22.

53. "Will Aleman Be Next President?" *Latinamerica Press*, 30 November 1995, 6.

Chapter Six

Dynamics of the Protestant Movement in Central America

Protestantism is a rebellion, a rebellion against the dominant Catholic culture.

> — Joseph Eldridge, United Methodist
> Church, former missionary to
> Honduras, Washington, D.C. 1990

We have asserted that Protestantism is a social movement in Central America, as supported by evidence from interviews, field research, surveys, and existing literature. To be an evangelical is to be part of a collectivity of now millions of people who, despite some differences, recognize a core of common interests and beliefs. As we saw in chapter 3, the movement has built-in cultural symbols or "frames" in the form of powerful biblical scriptures and music and spiritual experiences. These symbols have become widely familiar, forming communities of discourse through which movement members recognize each other and mobilize. This familiarity has helped the movement to spread through family and community networks—not demogoguery.

The opening quote presents the essence of Protestantism as a movement—sustained collective action, or "rebellion," against secularization and often against Catholicism. As we saw in chapter 4, one result of the movement has been a response from the Catholic Church in the form of confrontation, compromise, and cooperation with the evangelicals. Contentious interaction with Catholics is still predominant but more and more signs of compromise and cooperation are emerging. The Catholic Church has been shaken soundly from its complacency, and even if the ef-

fects of widespread Protestantism in Central America go no far-
ther than this, they already have been significant. However, the
effects involve much more than the Catholic response. The Protestant impact is evident not only in the countless numbers of Pentecostal communities but also in the highly tangible form of church
buildings, schools, clinics, seminaries, and development projects
scattered throughout Central America. In addition, we are witness-
ing embryonic political activism.

In chapter 5 we examined variations in the emerging political
influence of Protestants in Guatemala and Nicaragua. We found
that the Protestants in Nicaragua, including Pentecostals, appear
to be especially politicized when compared to the neighboring
countries. For instance, a quantitative study of Protestants in El
Salvador concluded that "most Protestants do not endorse an especially assertive church, one that intervenes on behalf of the poor
or mediates social conflicts. Only 24 to 42 percent of Protestants
feel comfortable with a vision of the church that seeks to restructure human society."[1] In Guatemala, other than the middle class
neo-Pentecostals, probably a smaller percentage of evangelicals
would endorse a church directly engaged in national politics. Yet
in Nicaragua church leaders *often* "intervene on behalf of the poor"
and mediate social conflicts through peace commissions, and now
three evangelical parties explicitly hope to "restructure human
society." What factors account for such differences in Protestant
politicization?

We propose that the level and type of Protestant political involvement is shaped by the interaction of missionary patterns, leadership development, and national political culture. Thus the
missionary patterns in Nicaragua were revised by the 1979 revolution and the subsequent war with the contras, which led to the
exit of many U.S. groups with reputations for political conservatism (sometimes to neighboring Honduras). Nicaragua has fewer
missionaries per capita than its neighbors, and the larger groups
that remain are generally from progressive and ecumenical denominations that have encouraged cooperation with Pentecostals and
even with many Catholics. They have also encouraged leadership
development through institutions that provide education, research,
and service. Having survived the changes to the religious fabric
brought by the revolution, the Protestant movement in Nicaragua
now has clearly moved into a phase of consolidation and institu-

tionalization by *Nicaraguan* leaders. Missionary patterns in Guatemala, on the other hand, began with Presbyterians but in recent decades have been dominated consistently by Pentecostals and neo-Pentecostals. During the 1980s the faith missions in Guatemala were crudely manipulated for the sake of Cold War politics by the U.S. government and by their own military establishments. This period has left lasting scars on many evangelicals who want to withdraw from national politics and from the mistrust that the manipulation engendered in communities. Furthermore, the Pentecostals are traditionally less institutionalized and less interested in politics than the ecumenical Protestants, and their inexperience shows.

As for the overall political culture, the people of Guatemala lack the experience of a successful revolution or a strong democracy, and the population is so apathetic about national politics that only a declining minority bothers to vote. Among Protestants in Guatemala the ecumenical churches and the neo-Pentecostals are trying to exert political influence at a national level, but they are the minority. Political activism is more likely to occur in Guatemala currently at the local level. The virtue of community participation is a commonly heard theme throughout Latin America.[2] Protestants are clearly active in their church communities, and they have also been known to challenge local government officials regarding corruption. This is grassroots activism that offers only gradual impact on the larger society, but it is activism nevertheless. One can envision strong alliances forming between Protestants and various local movements pushing for change, such as the indigenous, human rights, labor, and environmental movements.

In contrast, the political culture in Nicaragua is highly politicized already, and many Protestants are in the thick of it. In that country people are accustomed to reading about religious leaders on editorial pages and to seeing them in political office, such as the Catholic priests who served in the Sandinista Cabinet, the Baptists who served in the National Assembly, and several Protestant mayors. Over one hundred Protestant denominations are active in Nicaragua. About 60 percent of them are Pentecostal, and an even larger percentage are poor. In a country with a declining standard of living and almost 40 percent unemployment, evangelicals feel that they have been ill-served by the revolutionary government and by Chamorro's administration. Thus the evangelicals are not at present a monolithic voting bloc, either for the left or for the right. They are also inexperienced in politics, which is a reality that will lessen their impact on the 1996 elections. However, Protestants in Nicaragua have lived through dramatic political change from Somoza to the Sandinistas to neoliberalism—changes that seem to have encouraged openness to political possibilities rather than fatalism. They also have role models who are respected in political as well as religious circles, plus a network of supportive institutions and an amazing sense of faith. The Protestant movement has moved far beyond its missionary past. As we approach the millenium, Protestantism in Nicaragua will be more and more a political force with a power and momentum all its own.

Protestantism has the resources of what Tarrow calls "flexible mobilizing structures."[3] These structures are not only the original founding mission bodies but much more importantly, the individual churches themselves and the nationalized seminaries, research institutions, and umbrella organizations. Tarrow's emphasis on the value of flexibility for these structes is validated by the particular success of highly flexible "faith missions" and Pentecostal churches that can be formed virtually overnight. However, for the mobilizing structures to move into the realm of political change, perhaps in the form of religious political parties, requires a genuine opening of political opportunities. So far this is happening more noticeably in Nicaragua, and Nicaragua shows us that it is a serious mistake to assume automatially that evangelicals are rightists or supporters of the status quo. Whether Protestant activism will cut to the political left or the right, or whether it will arise at all, depends on the political culture and the leadership in each national context.

The Protestant movement has entered an important phase of consolidation and nationalization that presents its own challenges of holding members and sustaining spontaneity and fervor. It is likely that Protestant growth rates will slow as the movement becomes more focused on developing support institutions and less dedicated to recruitment. Furthermore, at this consolidation stage, the emerging national institutions of the Protestant movement are defining their own identity and this is often a conflictual process. For instance, the Presbyterian organization in

Guatemala is bitterly divided into conservative and progressive factions, even to the point of litigation. Similarly, leaders in the Baptist offices in San Salvador are arguing over denominational resources and we have already examined the fissure that occurred within CEPAD in Nicaragua. Such institutional strife appears to be an inherent aspect of this stage of social movement development. We assert however, that religious symbolism and rituals and faith are particularly resilient, even in the face of bureaucracy, dissension, and secular diversion.

It must be stressed that the resilience of this movement depends on it being authentically *of the people*, not an external imposition or an ideology that intellectuals might construct. Thus the true movement aspect of Protestantism was not realized until it became localized and more Pentecostal. The original missionaries provided the catalyst and the initial tools for the movement, but Protestantism in Central America has moved beyond missionaries. The believers continue to develop their own recruitment methods, framing symbols and mobilizing structures. If opportunities widen in their particular political culture, Protestants have shown that they can form alliances with other groups for political change. Such alliances include the ecumenical groups in Nicaragua, and exist even in Guatemala where activist women groups worked with evangelicals to form the fledgling FDNG political party.[4]

One Central American researcher sought to explain the potential of the evangelical belief system this way: "Pentecostal theological discourse is not very complex, but it speaks to the people who are uprooted. It offers participation in God's power. In a powerless population, Pentecostals offer power."[5] Predicting how that power will unfold in the future will require careful scrutiny at the microlevel. But it has already forever expanded the religious, cultural, and political landscape of Central America.

NOTES

1. Kenneth M. Coleman et al. "Protestantism in El Salvador: Conventional Wisdom versus the Survey Evidence," in *Rethinking Protestantism in Latin America*, ed. Virginia Garrard-Burnett and David Stoll (Philadelphia: Temple University Press, 1993), 131.

2. See Sheldon Annis, "Can Small-Scale Development Be Large-

Scale Policy?" in *Direct to the Poor: Grassroots Development in Latin America*, ed. Sheldon Annis and Peter Hakim (Boulder, Colo.: Lynne
Rienner, 1988), 209–18, for a cautious but optmistic discussion of the
eventually large-scale influence in Latin American nations exerted by
work at the community level. For a related analysis see the selections
in Minor Sinclair, ed., *The New Politics of Survival: Grassroots Movements in Central America* (New York: Monthly Review Press, 1995).

    3. Sidney Tarrow, *Power in Movement: Social Movements, Collec-
tive Action and Politics* (New York: Cambridge University Press, 1994),
142, 150.

    4. Regarding women in the Protestant movement, we refer the read-
er back to chapter 3, pages 53–61. Women are often leaders in Pentecostal as well as in the ecumenical, traditionalist churches. Cursory
observers often miss leadership development for women within Pentecostal churches where they are denied *nominal* leadership roles but are
often the authentic community and spiritual leaders. This leadership
development could carry over into the broader society. See Elizabeth
Brusco, "The Reformation of Machismo: Asceticism and Masculinity
among Colombian Evangelicals," in Virginia Garrard-Burnett and
David Stoll, eds., *Rethinking Protestantism in Latin America* (Pittsburgh: Temple University Press, 1993), 143–58.

    5. Jorge Bardeguez, research associate at the Antonio Valdivieso
Ecumenical Center (CAV), interview with author, Managua, Nicaragua, 9 November 1993.

References

Aguilar, Ernesto Paz. "The Origin and Development of Political Parties in Honduras." In *Political Parties and Democracy in Central America*, edited by Louis W. Goodman, William M LeoGrande, and Johanna Mendelson Forman. Boulder, Colo.: Westview 1990.

Alvarez, Carmelo, ed. *Pentecostalismo y Liberación: Una experiencia latinoamericana*. San José, Costa Rica: Departmento Ecumenico de Investigaciones, 1992.

Alvarez, Sonia E., and Arturo Escobar. "Conclusion: Theoretical and Political Horizons of Change in Contemporary Latin American Social Movements." In *The Making of Social Movements in Latin America*, edited by Arturo Escobar and Sonia Alvarez. Lanham, Md.: University Press of America, 1992.

Annis, Sheldon. *God and Production in a Guatemala Town*. Austin: University of Texas Press, 1987.

Annis, Sheldon and Peter Hakim, eds. *Direct to the Poor: Grassroots Development in Latin America*. Boulder, Colo.: Lynne Rienner, 1988.

Barry, Tom, and Deborah Preusch. *The Soft War: The Uses and Abuses of U.S. Economic Aid in Central America*. New York: Grove, 1988.

Berg, Mike and Paul Pretiz. *The Gospel People*. Monrovia, Calif.: WorldVision International/Latin America Mission, 1992.

Berryman, Phillip. *Liberation Theology: Essential Facts about the Revolutionary Movement in Latin America and Beyond*. New York: Pantheon, 1987.

———. *The Religious Roots of Rebellion: Christians in Central American Revolutions*. Maryknoll, N.Y.: Orbis, 1984.

Blanco, Gustavo, and Jaime Valverde. *Honduras: Iglesia y Cam-*

bio Social. San José, Costa Rica: Departmento Ecuménico de Investigaciones and Guaymuras, 1990.

Bonino, José Míguez, Carmelo Alvarez, and Roberto Craig. *Protestantismo y Liberalismo en America Latina*. 2d ed. San José, Costa Rica: Departmento Ecuménico de Investigaciones, 1985.

Brusco, Elizabeth. "The Reformation of Machismo: Asceticism and Masculinity among Colombian Evangelicals." In *Rethinking Protestantism in Latin America*, edited by Virginia Garrard-Burnett and David Stoll. Philadelphia: Temple University Press, 1993.

Budde, Michael L. *The Two Churches: Catholicism and Capitalism in the World-System*. Durham, N.C.: Duke University Press, 1990.

Burdick, John. *Looking for God in Brazil: The Progressive Catholic Church in Urban Brazil's Religious Arena*. Berkeley: University of California Press, 1993.

———. "Rethinking the Study of Social Movements: The Case of Christian Base Communities in Urban Brazil." In *The Making of Social Movements in Latin America: Identity, Strategy, and Democracy*, edited by Arturo Escobar and Sonia E. Alvarez. Boulder, Colo.: Westview, 1993.

Burns, Bradford E. *At War in Nicaragua: The Reagan Doctrine and the Politics of Nostalgia*. New York: Harper and Row, 1987.

Calderon, Fernando, Alejandro Piscitelli, and José Luis Reyna. "Social Movements: Actors, Theories, Expectations." In *The Making of Social Movements in Latin America: Identity, Strategy, and Democracy*, edited by Arturo Escobar and Sonia E. Alvarez. Boulder, Colo.: Westview, 1992.

Campbell, Gary, Director of Centro Ecumenico Antonio Valdivieso de la Estatua Jose Marti (CAV). Interview with author, Managua, Nicaragua, 8 November 1993.

Casco, Miguel Angel, President of Concilio Evangélico de Promoción and Renovación Social and founder of Movimiento Evangelico Popular (MEP). Interview with author, Managua, Nicaragua, 12 November 1993.

Casper, Gretchen. *Fragile Democracies: The Legacies of Authoritarian Rule*. Pittsburgh: University of Pittsburgh Press, 1995.

Clawson, David. "Religious Allegiance and Economic Development in Rural Latin America." *Journal of Interamerican Studies and World Affairs* 26 (November 1984): 499–524.

Cockburn, Leslie. *Out of Control: The Story of the Reagan Administration's Secret War in Nicaragua, the Illegal Arms Pipeline, and the Contra Drug Connection.* New York: Atlantic Montly Press, 1987.

Colby, Gerard, and Charlotte Dennett. *Thy Will Be Done: The Conquest of the Amazon: Nelson Rockefeller and Evangelism in the Age of Oil.* New York: HarperCollins, 1995.

Coleman, Kenneth M., et al. "Protestantism in El Salvador: Conventional Wisdom versus the Survey Evidence." In *Rethinking Protestantism in Latin America*, edited by Virginia Garrard-Burnett and David Stoll. Philadelphia: Temple University Press, 1993.

Cortés, Benjamín, Secretary General, Centro InterEclesial de Estudios Teológicos y Sociales (CIEETS). Interview with author, Managua, Nicaragua, 12 November 1993.

Crahan, Margaret. "Revolution and Counterrevolution: The Role of the Religious Right in Central America." In *The Right and Democracy in Latin America*, edited by Douglas A. Chalmers, Maria do Carmo Campello de Souza and Atilio A. Boron. New York: Praeger, 1992.

———. "Religion and Democratization in Central America." In *Political Parties and Democracy in Central America*, edited by Louis W. Goodman, William M. LeoGrande, and Johanna Mendelson Forman. Boulder, Colo.: Westview, 1992.

Daniels, Eugene. *A Protestant Looks at the Catholic Church in Mission.* Monrovia, Calif.: Mission Advanced Research Center, World Vision International, 1993.

Danner, Mark. "The Truth of El Mozote." *The New Yorker*, 6 December 1993, 50-133.

Daudelin, Jean, and W. E. Hewitt. "Latin American Politics: Exit the Catholic Church?" In *Organized Religion in the Political Transformation of Latin America*, edited by Satya R. Pattnayak Lanham, Md.: University Press of America, 1995.

Deiros, Pablo A. "Protestant Fundamentalism in Latin America." In *Fundamentalisms Observed*, edited by Martin E. Marty and R. Scott Appleby. Illinois: University of Chicago Press, 1991.

Diamond, Sara. *Spiritual Warfare: The Politics of the Christian Right*. Boston: South End, 1989.

Dixon, David. "The New Protestantism in Latin America: Remembering What We Already Know, Testing What We Have Learned." *Comparative Politics* (July 1995): 471–92.

Dodson, Michael. "Shifting Patterns of Religious Influence in Central America: The Case of Revolutionary Nicaragua." Paper presented at the American Political Science Association Meeting. Chicago, Illinois, September 1992.

Dodson, Michael, and Laura Nuzzi O'Shaughnessy. *Nicaragua's Other Revolution: Religious Faith and Political Struggle*. Chapel Hill: University of North Carolina Press, 1990.

Drogus, Carol Ann. "The Rise and Decline of Liberation Theology: Churches, Faith, and Political Change in Latin America." *Comparative Politics* (July 1995): 465–77.

Eldridge, Joseph. United Methodist Church. Interview with author, Washington, D.C., 8 June 1990.

Equizábal, Cristina. "Parties, Programs, and Politics in El Salvador." In *Political Parties and Democracy in Central America*, edited by Louis W. Goodman, William M. LeoGrande, and Johanna Mendelson Forman. Boulder, Colo.: Westview, 1990.

Escobar, Arturo. "Culture, Economics, and Politics in Latin American Social Movements Theory and Reasearch." In *The Making of Social Movements in Latin America*, edited by Arturo Escobar and Sonia E. Alvarez. Lanham, Md.: University Press of America, 1992.

Ezcurra, Ana Maria. *The Neoconservative Offensive: U.S. Churches and Ideological Struggle for Latin America*. New York: Circus Publications, 1986.

Falla, Richard. *Massacres in the Jungle: Ixcan, Guatemala, 1975-1982*. Boulder, Colo.: Westview Press, 1994.

Farah, Douglas. "The Lost Decade: Central America Is Staggering under Its '80s Legacy." *The Washington Post National Weekly Edition*, 14–20 June 1993, 6–8.

Froehle, Brian. "The Catholic Church and Politics in Venezuela." In *Conflict and Competition: The Latin American Church in a Changing Environment*, edited by Edward L. Cleary and Hannah Stewart-Gambino. Boulder, Colo.: Lynne Rienner, 1992.

Fuentes, Bishop Eduardo. Interview with author, Panajachel, Guatemala, 7 July 1990.

Garrard-Burnett, Virginia. "Conclusion: Is This Latin America's Reformation?" In *Rethinking Protestantism in Latin America*, edited by Virginia Garrard-Burnett and David Stoll. Philadelphia: Temple University Press, 1993.

———. "Protestantism in Rural Guatemala, 1872–1954." *Latin American Research Review* 24, no.2 (1989): 127–42.

Garst, Rachel and Tom Barry. *Feeding the Crisis: U.S. Food Aid and Farm Policy in Central America*. Lincoln: University of Nebraska Press, 1990.

Gill, Anthony. "Rendering Unto Caesar? Religious Competition and Catholic Political Strategy in Latin America, 1962–79." *American Journal of Political Science* 38 (May 1994): 403–25.

Gill, Lesley. "Like a Veil to Cover Them: Women and the Pentecostal Movement in La Paz." *American Ethnologist* 17, no. 4 (1990): 708–21.

Giron, Padre Andres. Interview with author, Nueve Concepcion, Guatemala, 14 June 1990.

Goldin, Liliana R. and B. Metz. "An Expression of Cultural Change: Invisible Converts to Protestantism among Highland Guatemala Mayas." *Ethnology* 30, no. 4 (1991): 325–38.

Green, Linda. "Shifting Affliliations: Mayan Widows and Evangelicos in Guatemala." In *Rethinking Protestantism in Latin America*, edited by Virginia Garrard-Burnett and David Stoll. Philadelphia: Temple University Press, 1993.

Greenway, Roger S. "Protestant Missionary Activity in Latin America." In *Coming of Age: Protestantism in Contemporary Latin America*, edited by Daniel R. Miller. Lanham, Md.: University Press of America, 1994.

Hall, John, Professor of Religious Studies, Nazarene Seminario. Interview with author, San José, Costa Rica, 8 July 1993.

Hertzke, Allen D. *Representing God in Washington: The Role of Religious Lobbies in the American Polity*. Knoxville: University of Tennessee Press, 1988.

Honey, Martha, and Tony Avigran. "The CIA's War." *Nation,* 6 February 1988.

Inter-Hemispheric Education Resource Center. *Private Organizations with U.S. Connections—El Salvador: Directory and Analysis*. Albuquerque: The Resource Center, 1988.

————. *Private Organizations with U.S. Connections—Guatemala: Directory and Analysis*. Albuquerque: The Resource Center, 1988.

————. *Private Organizations with U.S. Connections—Honduras: Directory and Analysis*. Albuquerque: The Resource Center, 1988.

Ireland, Rowan. *Kingdoms Come: Religion and Politics in Brazil*. Pittsburgh: University of Pittsburgh Press, 1991.

Jabine, Thomas B., and Richard P. Claude, eds. *Human Rights and Statistics*. Philadelphia: University of Pennsylvania Press, 1992.

Jeffrey, Paul. "Telling the Truth: Church Project in Guatemala." *Christian Century*, 30 August–6 September 1995.

————. "Base Communities Struggling in Nicaragua." *Latinamerica Press*, 4 March 1993.

Kanagy, Conrad L. "The Formation and Development of a Protestant Conversion Movement among the Highland Quichua of Ecuador." *Sociological Analysis* 51 (summer 1990): 205–17.

Keogh, Dermot, ed. *Church and Politics in Latin America*. New York: St. Martins, 1990.

Kessler, John. *500 Anos de evangelizacion en America Latina desde una perspectiva evangelica*. San José, Costa Rica: Departamento de Publicaciones del Instituto Internacional de Evangelizacion a Fondo, 1992.

Kirk, John M. *Politics and the Catholic Church in Nicaragua*. Gainesville: University of Florida Press, 1990.

Kolbenschlag, Madonna-Claire. "The Protestant Ethic and Evangelical Capitalism: The Weberian Thesis Revisited." *Southern Quarterly*, 14 July 1976, 287–306.

Lalive d'Epinay, Christian. *Haven to the Masses: A Study of the Pentecostal Movement in Chile*. London: Lutterworth, 1969.

LeoGrande, William M. "Political Parties and Postrevolutionary Politics in Nicaragua." In *Political Parties and Democracy in Central America*, edited by Louis W. Goodman, William M. LeoGrande, and Johanna Mendelson Forman Boulder, Colo.: Westview, 1992.

Lernoux, Penny. *People of God: The Struggle for World Catholicism*. New York: Viking, 1989.

Levine, Daniel H. "Religious Change, Empowerment and Power: Reflections on Latin American Experience." In *Organized Religion in the Political Transformation of Latin America*, edited by Satya R. Pattnayak. Lanham, Md.: University Press of America, 1995.

———. *Popular Voices in Latin American Catholicism.* Princeton: Princeton University Press, 1990.

Levine, Daniel H., ed. *Religion and Political Conflict in Latin America.* Chapel Hill: University of North Carolina Press, 1986.

Levine, Daniel H. "Religion and Politics in Comparative and Historical Perspective." *Comparative Politics* 19, no. 1 (1986): 95–122.

Lewis, Norman. *The Missionaries.* New York: McGraw-Hill, 1988.

Loeb, David. "Self-Coup/Counter-Coup: Serrano Is Out: What Comes Next?" *Report on Guatemala* 14 (summer 1993).

Luttwak, Edward. "The Missing Dimension." In *Religion, The Missing Dimension of Statecraft*, edited by Douglas Johnston and Cynthia Sampson. New York: Oxford University Press, 1994.

Lynch, Edward A. *Religion and Politics in Latin America: Liberation Theology and Christian Democracy.* New York: Praeger, 1991.

Madrid, Edmundo Morales, President of Alianza Evangelica de Guatemala. Interview with author, Guatemala City, Guatemala, 9 July 1990.

Mainwaring, Scott. *The Catholic Church and Politics in Brazil, 1916–1985.* Stanford, Calif.: Stanford University Press, 1986.

Mainwaring, Scott, and Alexander Wilde, eds. *The Progressive Church in Latin America.* Indiana: University of Notre Dame Press, 1983.

Mariz, Cecilia Loreto. *Coping with Poverty: Pentecostals and Christian Base Communities in Brazil.* Philadelphia: Temple University Press, 1994.

Martin, David. *Tongues of Fire: The Explosion of Protestantism in Latin America.* London: Blackwell, 1990.

McGovern, Arthur F. *Liberation Theology and Its Critics: Toward an Assessment.* Maryknoll, N.Y.: Orbis, 1989.

Miller, Daniel R. ed. *Coming of Age: Protestantism in Contem-*

porary Latin America. Lanham, Md.: University Press of America, 1994.

Minerva, Otto. Academic Vice President, Seminario Biblio Latinoamericano. Interview with author, San José, Costa Rica, 26 July 1993.

Montt, General Efraín Ríos. Interview with author, Guatemala City, Guatemala, 14 July 1990.

Morley, Morris H. *Washington, Somoza and the Sandinistas*. New York: Cambridge University Press, 1994.

———. *The Reagan Administration and Nicaragua: How Washington Constructs Its Case for Counterrevolution in Central America*. New York: Institute for Media Analysis, 1987.

Mulligan, Joseph E. *The Nicaraguan Church and the Revolution*. Kansas City, Mo.: Sheed and Ward, 1991.

Muratorio, Blanca. "Protestantism and Capitalism Revisited in the Rural Highlands of Ecuador." *Journal of Peasant Studies* 8 (October 1980): 37–60.

Nichols, Bruce. "Religious Conciliation between the Sandinistas and the East Coast Indians of Nicaragua." In *Religion, The Missing Dimension of Statecraft*, edited by Douglas Johnston and Cynthia Sampson. New York: Oxford University Press, 1994.

Nuncio, Enrique. Director of Campus Crusade for Christ. Interview with author, San Salvador, El Salvador, 19 January 1995.

O'Shaughnessy, Laura Nuzzi. "Onward Christian Soldiers: The Case of Protestantism in Central America." In *Religious Resurgence and Politics in the Contemporary World*, edited by Emile Sahliyeh. Albany: State University of New York Press, 1990.

Parajon, Gustavo Adolfo. Executive Director, Comite Evangelico Pro-Ayuda Al Desarrollo (CEPAD). Interview with author, Managua, Nicaragua, November 1993.

Pattnayak, Satya R. "Social Change, Political Competition, and Religious Innovation in Latin America: An Introduction." In *Organized Religion in the Political Transformation of Latin America*, edited by Satya R. Pattnayak, Lanham, Md.: University Press of America, 1995.

———. "Appendix: The Institutional Capacity of the Catholic Church: An Evaluation." In *Organized Religion in the Politi-*

cal Transformation of Latin America, edited by Satya R. Pattnayak. Lanham, Md.: University Press of America, 1995.

Perera, Victor. *Unfinished Conquest: The Guatemalan Tragedy.*
Berkeley: University of California Press, 1993.

Peterson, Roy. Director of External Relations, Summer Institute
of Linguistics (Guatemala Branch of Wycliffe Bible Translators). Interview with author, Guatemala City, Guatemala, 2
November 1993.

Pixley, Jorge. Professor of Bible at Seminario Bautista. Interview
with author, Managua, Nicaragua, 10 November 1993.

Pottenger, John R. *The Political Theory of Liberation Theology:
Toward a Reconvergence of Social Values and Social Science.*
Albany: State University of New York Press, 1986.

Poythress, Vern S. *Understanding Dispensationalists.* Grand Rapids, Mich.: Zondervan, 1987.

Prendes, Jorge Caceres. "Political Radicalization and Popular
Pastoral Practices in El Salvador, 1969–1985." In *The Progressive Church in Latin America*, edited by Scott Mainwaring and Alexander Wilde. Indiana: University of Notre Dame
Press, 1983.

Ptacek, Kerry. "U.S. Protestants and Liberation Theology." *Orbis*
(fall 1986): 433–41.

"The Rise of the Religious Right in Central America." *Resource
Center Bulletin* 10 (summer/fall 1987).

Robinson, William I. *David and Goliath: The U.S. War against
Nicaragua.* New York: Monthly Review Press, 1987.

Rose, Susan D., and Steve Brouwer. "The Export of Fundamentalist Americanism: U.S. Evangelical Education in Guatemala." *Latin American Perspectives* (fall 1990): 42–56.

Sanneh, Lamin. "Global Christianity and the re-education of the
West." *Christian Century*, 19–26 July 1995, 715.

Schultze, Quentin J. "Orality and Power in Latin American Pentecostalism." In *Coming of Age: Protestantism in Contemporary Latin America*, edited by Daniel R. Miller. Lanham, Md.:
University Press of America, 1994.

Serrano, Jorge Serrano. Interview with author, Guatemala City,
Guatemala. 9 July 1990.

Seligson, Mitchell A. and Joel M. Jutkowitz. *Guatemalan Values
and the Prospects for Democratic Development.* Development

Associates/University of Pittsburgh/Asociacion de Investigacion y Estudios Sociales (ASIES), 1994.

Sexton, James D. "Protestantism and Modernization in Two Guatemalan Towns." *American Ethnologist* 5 (May 1978): 280–302.

Sherman, Amy L. "And Be Ye Transformed: Christian Orthodoxy and Socio-Economic Transformation in Guatemala." Ph.D. diss., University of Virginia, 1995.

Siewert, John A., and John A. Kenyon, eds. *Mission Handbook: 1993–95*. Monrovia, Calif.: Mission Advanced Research Center, WorldVision International, 1995.

Sigmund, Paul. *Liberation Theology at the Crossroads: Democracy or Revolution?* New York: Oxford University Press, 1990.

Sklar, Holly. *Washington's War on Nicaragua*. Boston: South End Press, 1988.

Smith, Alexa. "Presbyterians Sought as International Witnesses to Guatemalan Violence." *The News of the Presbyterian Church U.S.A.*, September 1995.

Smith, Dennis A. "The Gospel According to the United States: Evangelical Broadcasting in Central America." In *American Evangelicals and the Mass Media*, edited by Quentin J. Schultze. Grand Rapids, Mich.: Zondervan, 1990.

Smith, Dennis A. Latin American Evangelical Center for Pastoral Studies (CELEP). Interviews with author, Guatemala City, Guatemala, 1990, 1993, 1994, 1995.

Smith, Peter H. "Crisis and Democracy in Latin America." *World Politics* 43 (July 1991): 608–34.

Snow, David, Burke E. Rochford, Jr., Steven K. Worden, and Robert D. Benford. "Frame Alignment Processes, Micromobilization, and Movement Participation." *American Sociological Review* 51 (1986): 464–81.

Stewart-Gambino, Hannah. "Introduction: New Game, New Rules." In *Conflict and Competition: The Latin American Church in a Changing Environment*, edited by Edward L. Cleary and Hannah Stewart-Gambino. Boulder, Colo.: Lynne Rienner, 1992.

Stoll, David. "'Jesus is Lord of Guatemala': Evangelical Reform in a Death-Squad State." In *Accounting for Fundamentalisms: The Dynamic Character of Movements*, edited by Martin E. Marty and R. Scott Appleby. Illinois: University of Chicago Press, 1994.

References   145

———. *Is Latin America Turning Protestant? The Politics of Evangelical Growth*. Berkeley: University of California Press, 1990.

———. *Fishers of Men or Founders of Empire? The Wycliffe Bible Translators in Latin America*. Cambridge, Mass.: Cultural Survival Quarterly/Zed Press, 1983.

Swanson, Jeffrey. *Echoes of the Call: Identity and Ideology among American Missionaries in Ecuador*. New York: Oxford University Press, 1995.

Tarrow, Sidney. *Power in Movement: Social Movements, Collective Action and Politics*. New York: Cambridge University Press, 1994.

Thornton, Philip W. "Resocialization: Roman Catholics Becoming Protestants in Colombia, South America." *Anthropological Quarterly* 57 (January 1984): 28–38.

Turner, Paul R. "Religious Conversion and Community Development." *Journal for the Scientific Study of Religion* 18 (September 1979): 252–60.

U.N. Development Programme. *Human Development Report 1993*. New York: United Nations, 1993.

Vargas Llosa, Alvaro, and Santiago Aroca. *Riding the Tiger: Ramiro de Leon Carpio's Battle for Human Rights in Guatemala*. Miami: Brickell Communications, 1995.

Walker, Thomas W. *Reagan versus the Sandinistas: The Undeclared War on Nicaragua*. Boulder, Colo.: Westview, 1987.

Weber, Timothy P. "Dispensationalism." In *A New Handbook of Christian Theology*, edited by Donald W. Musser and J.L. Price. Nashville: Abingdon, 1992.

Weber, Max. *The Protestant Ethic and the Spirit of Capitalism*. New York: Scribner's, 1958 [1930].

Wheaton, Phillip. Telephone interview with author, 20 September 1993.

Wheeler, Dennis. Director of PAVA and owner of Dona Luisa's Restaurant. Interview with author, Antigua, Guatemala. 25 January 1993.

Whitman, Dale. Christian Missionary Alliance. Interview with author, DeLand, Florida. 15 and 20 November 1995.

Willems, Emilio. *Followers of the New Faith: Culture Change and the Rise of Protestantism in Brazil and Chile*. Nashville: Vanderbilt University Press, 1967.

Williams, Philip J. *The Catholic Church and Politics in Nicaragua and Costa Rica*. Pittsburgh: University of Pittsburgh Press, 1989.

Williams, Rhys H. "Movement Dynamics and Social Change: Transforming Fundamentalist Ideology and Organizations." In *Accounting for Fundamentalisms: The Dynamic Character of Movements*, edited by Martin E. Marty and R. Scott Appleby. Illinois: The University of Chicago Press, 1994.

Wink, Walter. *Engaging the Powers: Discernment and Resistance in a World of Domination*. Minneapolis: Fortress, 1992.

Wuthnow, Robert, and Matthew P. Lawson. "Sources of Christian Fundamentalism in the United States." In *Accounting for Fundamentalisms: The Dynamic Character of Movements*, edited by Martin E. Marty and R. Scott Appleby. Illinois: University of Chicago Press, 1994.

———. "The Future of the Religious Right." In *No Longer Exiles: The Religious New Right in American Politics*, edited by Michael Cromartie. Washington, D.C.: Ethics and Public Policy Center, 1993.

———. *The Restructuring of American Religion: Society and Faith Since World War II*. Princeton, N.J.: Princeton University Press, 1988.

Zamora, Ruben. FDR Party Member, and Vice President of National Assembly during Cristiani's presidency. Interview with author, San Salvador, El Salvador, 19 January 1993.

Zub, Roberto Kurylowicz. *Protestantismo y Elecciones en Nicaragua*. Managua, Nicaragua: Centro InterEclesial de Estudios Teologicos y Sociales, 1993.

Index

About the Author

Anne Motley Hallum is an associate professor of political science at Stetson University where she teaches religion and politics. She received her doctorate in political science from Vanderbilt University. She is currently conducting research about grass-roots environmentalism in Guatemala.

She is also the Founder and Chair of the Board of Directors of The Alliance for International Reforestation, Inc. (A.I.R.), a community-based environmental organization working in over thirty villages in Guatemala. A.I.R. is a tax-deductible non-profit organization, with U.S. "headquarters" in the Political Science Department at Stetson University, DeLand, Florida.